MODERN
TANKS

MODERN TANKS

60 years of armoured fighting vehicles: an illustrated A–Z of tanks, armoured vehicles, tank destroyers, command versions and specialized tanks from 1945 to the present day

GEORGE FORTY

southwater

This edition is published by Southwater

Southwater is an imprint of Anness Publishing Ltd
Hermes House, 88–89 Blackfriars Road, London SE1 8HA
tel. 020 7401 2077; fax 020 7633 9499
www.southwaterbooks.com; www.annesspublishing.com

If you like the images in this book and would like to investigate using them for publishing, promotions or advertising,
please visit our website www.practicalpictures.com for more information.

© Anness Publishing Ltd 2007, 2008

UK agent: The Manning Partnership Ltd; tel. 01225 478444; fax 01225 478440; sales@manning-partnership.co.uk
UK distributor: Grantham Book Services Ltd; tel. 01476 541080; fax 01476 541061; orders@gbs.tbs-ltd.co.uk
North American agent/distributor: National Book Network; tel. 301 459 3366; fax 301 429 5746; www.nbnbooks.com
Australian agent/distributor: Pan Macmillan Australia; tel. 1300 135 113; fax 1300 135 103; customer.service@macmillan.com.au
New Zealand agent/distributor: David Bateman Ltd; tel. (09) 415 7664; fax (09) 415 8892

A CIP catalogue record for this book is available from the British Library.

Publisher: Joanna Lorenz
Project Editor: Felicity Forster
Copy Editor and Indexer: Tim Ellerby

Cover Design: Jonathan Davison
Designer: Design Principals
Production Controller: Wendy Lawson

Previously published as part of a larger volume, *The World Encyclopedia of Tanks*

ETHICAL TRADING POLICY
Because of our ongoing ecological investment programme, you, as our customer, can have the pleasure and reassurance of
knowing that a tree is being cultivated on your behalf to naturally replace the materials used to make the book you are holding.
For further information about this scheme, go to www.annesspublishing.com/trees

PAGE 1: **Challenger 1 Main Battle Tank.** PAGE 2: **T-62 Main Battle Tank.**
PAGE 3: **M60 Main Battle Tank.** BELOW: **Strv 103 S Main Battle Tank.**

Contents

Introduction

What is a tank? Expressed in its simplest terms, a tank can be defined as a means of transporting firepower about on the battlefield, with its weapon system and crew protected from direct enemy fire. This revolutionary weapon has been in existence for under a hundred years, and in that time it has become one of the most important and indispensable components of the battle-winning All Arms Team. The tank is just one of the many types of Armoured Fighting Vehicle (AFV) found on the modern battlefield. What makes it special is the careful blend of its three basic characteristics – firepower, protection and mobility – into a lethal mix that can bring instantaneous, accurate, direct fire to bear, whenever and wherever it is needed, day and night, whether on the move or stationary. These three characteristics can be blended together in differing amounts to produce very different results, as can be seen in the directory section of this book.

Firepower is undoubtedly the most important characteristic because it is a tank's reason for being. The type and size of weapon system can vary enormously, and as this becomes larger and more sophisticated, the carrying vehicle invariably increases in both size and weight as there is more to protect.

If a tank is to achieve its mission, then an effective means of protection is vital. Although this can be achieved in a variety of ways, the basis is usually some form of armour plate composed of steel, aluminium, plastic-sandwich, ceramic, reactive or other materials, which inevitably increases the

TOP: **Firepower. Challenger MBTs of A Squadron, 1st Royal Tank Regiment, night-firing on Castlemartin Ranges, Pembrokeshire, Wales, 2001.**
ABOVE: **Protection. The massively thick, advanced Chobham type armour on the hull and turret of this Abrams M1A1 MBT gives protection against ATGWs (Anti-Tank Guided Weapons) and other battlefield weapons.**

tank's size and weight. Main Battle Tanks (MBTs) of today weigh around 60–70 tons, including much weighty armour. There are also other ways of providing protection, such as limiting size, lowering silhouette, camouflaging the tell-tale shape and using aids such as local smoke to help it "disappear". Inevitably as the tank's protection has become more and more sophisticated, so too have the anti-tank weapons ranged against it. Therefore its protection must be able to deal with all manner of attacks,

LEFT: **River crossing. Royal Engineers have constructed this Class 80 ferry, to practise ferrying a Challenger 2 during training at Bovington, Dorset, England.**
BELOW: **Mobility. A Challenger 2, belonging to the Armour Centre at Bovington, Dorset, England, powers its way effortlessly through thick mud on the training area.**

from ground level – such as mines – through a vast range of hand-held/vehicle-borne guns and guided missiles that can attack at any level, to specific top-attack weapons. As far as possible, it must also now protect against nuclear, biological and chemical weapons. To all of this must be added a tank's deadliest foe – another tank, with its weapon system firing more and more sophisticated ammunition specifically designed to penetrate armour.

Mobility is the third vital characteristic, and again as the tank has become larger and heavier, increasingly more powerful powerplant, transmission and suspension are needed to move it over all types of terrain. Cross-country, the track clearly wins over the wheel, and good mobility is essential if the tank is to achieve its varying missions. Weight affects its portability, especially by air or over water. MBTs have probably now reached their ultimate size and weight, and so there is now a trend towards lighter, smaller, more portable tanks. This in turn puts the smaller tank at a distinct disadvantage in any tank versus tank engagements, when faced with a larger, better protected and better armed enemy, so tank development can be a vicious circle.

This book contains a selection of tanks from 1945 to the present day. We have deliberately confined our coverage to the more important and interesting models worldwide, so while it is definitely not an exhaustive encyclopedia of modern tanks, it will give the reader a good indication of what the modern tank is all about. In the hands of well-trained, highly professional soldiers, the awesome power of the tank still lives on and will continue to do so into the foreseeable future. FEAR NAUGHT!

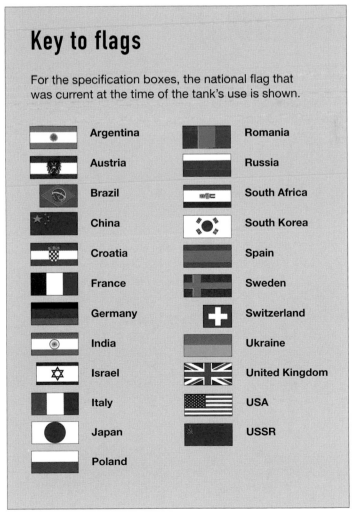

Key to flags

For the specification boxes, the national flag that was current at the time of the tank's use is shown.

	Argentina		Romania
	Austria		Russia
	Brazil		South Africa
	China		South Korea
	Croatia		Spain
	France		Sweden
	Germany		Switzerland
	India		Ukraine
	Israel		United Kingdom
	Italy		USA
	Japan		USSR
	Poland		

The History of Modern Tanks

The history of the tank has very largely been the history of 20th-century ground warfare, this revolutionary new weapon being conceived to help break the early battlefield stalemate of World War I. Later it had mixed fortunes in the years of peace following 1918, but came back into its own during World War II and has maintained its pre-eminent position ever since. Tanks have been produced in all shapes and sizes throughout their history. Nevertheless, without exception, they have all had the basic characteristics of firepower, protection and mobility. It is how these are balanced together that makes a critical difference to their effectiveness. During the tank's history some of its original roles have been taken over by other types of Armoured Fighting Vehicle (AFV). Nevertheless, the ability of the tank to carry firepower about on the battlefield with a protected crew and weapons has remained essential. We are now seeing a requirement for lighter AFVs to replace current Main Battle Tanks (MBTs), which poses the question whether the tank as we currently know it will still be with us by the end of the 21st century.

LEFT: **The Type 61 MBT was the first tank produced by Japan after World War II. After almost a decade in development, it ended a long period when Japan had no armaments industry.**

The Cold War

While there is no doubt that World War II had proved once again that tanks could win major battles, just as after World War I, the American and British armoured forces were reduced significantly to peacetime levels – 20 cavalry regiments and eight from the Royal Tank Regiment (RTR) respectively – the rest disbanded, despite worldwide commitments such as the dismantling of the British Empire. In addition, the spectre of nuclear war between the Super Powers hung over Europe, with NATO and the Warsaw Pact countries facing each other across the Iron Curtain. Bolstering up the Soviet threat to the West was a mass of armoured units that appeared ready to strike at any moment and whose purpose was to follow-up a pre-emptive nuclear strike. To guard against such an eventuality the US, UK and other NATO nations stationed many of their tank units in north-west Europe, or had complicated "Reforger" programmes in which the tanks were

ABOVE RIGHT: **On the other side of the Iron Curtain, American M60s, belonging to their armoured regiments stationed in West Germany, got on with their training for battle. These three are firing on the open range.** BELOW: **The Cold War was certainly cold on the eastern side of the Iron Curtain. Here Red Army soldiers on manoeuvres in the early 1950s use a platoon of T-34/76s to help them move through thick snow.**

kept in specially weatherproofed shelters in Europe while the crews were at home – ready to be flown out to man them at a moment's notice. Either way it was an expensive and time-consuming business, but the threat was real enough, both sides fearing that the other would strike first.

The "shield and sword" principle of NATO undoubtedly did much to prevent a third world war during the remainder of the 20th century. Had war occurred, tank battles would have been a major feature. Cracks in the Warsaw Pact were apparent from time to time, such as with the Hungarian uprising in October 1956, but these were savagely repressed,

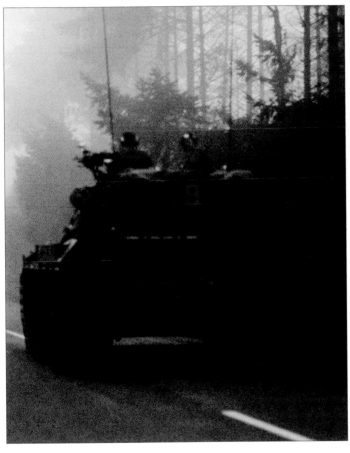

LEFT: **Guns rear, a column of M60s return to their barracks after manoeuvres in southern Germany. They are passing another armoured column led by an M113 APC.** BELOW LEFT: **Driving home in the morning mist. A German Leopard 1 returning to barracks at the end of an exercise through mist-shrouded pine forests.** BELOW: **NBC (Nuclear, Biological, Chemical) warfare was yet another feature of the Cold War, which required tank soldiers to wear special uniforms, including respirators, and to decontaminate their tanks. Here a German crew practise decontamination drills, with suitable detergent sprays.**

slowly starting up their own tank-building industry once again, but this time with very different objectives. It was soon clear that German tank-building expertise was as good as ever, clearly demonstrated by the Leopard 1 and later Leopard 2 tanks. For anyone stationed in Germany during the 1940s to the 1970s, this was a time of considerable change, encompassing initially an era of massive free-wheeling exercises that saw tanks running on their tracks over much of the countryside, and then of tactical training becoming more and more restricted as costs increased and land became more precious.

The training expedients that had to evolve are dealt with later in this book, but it is worth noting that as the lethality of tank gun ammunition increased, so too did the size of army firing-range danger areas in order to safeguard the public; alternatively, other methods of training tank gunners would have to evolve. Nevertheless, the threat of armoured conflict was always present, making this type of training essential at all levels.

There was also an important shift in some countries, such as Great Britain, for their armies to change from conscripts to regular soldiers, causing considerable changes to the training cycle of tank crews. In general terms, after some teething problems, this was to produce a far more professional and well motivated tank crewman, whose expertise has been evidenced in the last two Gulf Wars. Tanks were also becoming ever more sophisticated, requiring that the training of tank crewmen also had to develop and improve continually.

using in this case over 1,000 tanks to crush it. At the same time the whole world was becoming "awash" with tanks – the highly successful Soviet T series, for example, being widely available and mirroring the similar worldwide availability of such small arms as the AK-47 Kalashnikov assault rifle. NATO countries favoured the American M47, M48, M60 series or the British Centurion, all of which were produced in large numbers both at home for export and under licence abroad. Additionally, other "sleeping giants" like China had also begun to develop their own tank-building industry.

The Armies of Occupation in Germany gradually became less "occupying forces" and more equal partners as the erstwhile enemies were welcomed back into the fold, even

Korea and Vietnam

On June 25, 1950, Blitzkrieg struck again, this time in the Far East where a two-pronged assault, spearheaded by tanks, raced south across the 38th Parallel dividing North Korea from South Korea. Their success was stunning, although the North Korean Peoples Army (NKPA) based their armoured tactics more on those of the Red Army than of the *Panzerwaffe*. The South Koreans and the Americans, who were there as an army of occupation, could muster just a handful of M24 Chaffee light tanks, which the NKPA T-34s dealt with easily. Somehow, the Americans managed to hold on and regroup, bring in some Pershings and Shermans from Japan, and then one battalion of more modern M46 Pattons. By the third week in August, there were over 500 US tanks in the Pusan perimeter, and by early September, US tanks outnumbered the NKPA by at least five to one.

The United Nations forces (the defending force was now approved by the UN) soon went on to the offensive, driving the North Koreans back over the 38th Parallel and into North Korea. By now there were small numbers of both British and French tanks in the UN command, the British Centurion proving conclusively to be the best tank of the campaign. The war looked like drawing to a victorious close, but on November 25, 1950,

TOP: **Invasion! On the morning of June 25, 1950, some 10,000 North Korean infantry supported by more than 50 tanks (Soviet-built T-34/85s) swept across the 38th Parallel, spearheading the invasion of South Korea. They were followed by more troops and more tanks, and swiftly over-ran most of the country.** ABOVE: **Shermans of 2nd US Infantry Division blast enemy positions during an assault on the Chinese Communist Forces on the East Central Front in Korea, September 1951.**

the Chinese launched a massive offensive, the front not being stabilized until early April, back along the 38th Parallel. Thereafter, although tanks had shown themselves well able to operate in the rugged terrain, the use of armour both in attack and defence was sidelined and the war lapsed into an uneasy truce.

Since those days, the NKVA has built up a massive army containing over 6,500 tanks, half of which are main battle tanks of Russian or Chinese manufacture. South Korea has some 4,650 tanks, of which some 2,330 are also main battle tanks. The latter is tasked to absorb and then defeat any Blitzkrieg-type assault with prompt support from the US Army.

LEFT: **Sweeping for mines. An M48 tank with an automatic mine-sweeper checks the road from Cam Lo to Mai Loc, Vietnam, in the northern I Corps area near the Demilitarized Zone (DMZ), September 16, 1970.**
BELOW: **An M155 Sheridan tank belonging to Troop "A" of the 1st Battalion, 1st Cavalry Regiment, American Division, pauses beneath some trees about 30.6km/19 miles north of Tam Ky, Vietnam, March 18, 1970.**

Indo-China and Vietnam

The French fought a guerrilla war here from 1951–54 against the Viet Minh, in the end suffering a humiliating defeat at Dien Bien Phu, Vietnam. They used American World War II armour, including less than 500 tanks and tank destroyers spread over an area of some 72,520sq km/28,000sq miles. By comparison, when it came to be the Americans' turn to fight there, they employed some 600 tanks and over 2,000 other AFVs in an area less than one-third that size. A terrain study carried out in Vietnam by a team of US tankers in 1967 showed that nearly half the country could be traversed by AFVs all year round. Nevertheless, in the difficult areas like the Mekong Delta and the Central Highlands the lightly equipped, fast-moving Vietcong were far more capable of carrying out full-scale mobile war.

While the main American AFV used was the M113 (almost in the role of a light tank), M41s and later M48s were introduced as the war escalated. From 1967–68 the Australians sent a

squadron of medium tanks (British-built Centurions), and they fought a number of successful actions before being withdrawn from 1971–72. New equipment arriving in the late 1960s included the Sheridan Light Tank, with its wholly inappropriate 152mm/5.98in anti-tank missile that was never used in anger. Tank versus tank combat took place only twice: once at Ben Het in March 1969 between two tanks of US 69th Armour and a number of North Vietnam Army (NVA) PT-76s, two of which were knocked out; and in Laos in March 1971, where South Vietnamese M41s clashed with NVA tanks.

In their spring offensive in 1972, Viet Cong Russian-built T-54s and their Chinese equivalent Type 59s fought it out with American M48A3s of the South Vietnamese 20th Tank Regiment. Unfortunately the South Vietnamese not only let the initiative pass to the enemy, but also used their armour in a static role, inviting piecemeal destruction. Thus, as in Indo-China, a seemingly unsophisticated "peasant" army had shown itself better able to handle armour than its far more armour-conscious opponent.

LEFT: **USMC flamethrowing M67s (developed from the M48), burning fields in Vietnam, near the 1st Battalion, 3rd Regiment command post, 3rd Marine Division, January 1966.**

The uneasy peace

In addition to the Korean and Vietnam Wars, the 20th century saw many other conflicts taking place all over the world, for example on the Indian subcontinent, in the ever-turbulent Middle East, and even on the "roof of the world" in Afghanistan. Tanks have been employed in all of these wars, as the following four examples demonstrate.

India–Pakistan

Following World War II, the British Army found itself responsible not only for occupation duties in Europe but also for "Imperial Policing" in the British Empire as trouble flared in Palestine, then Malaya, Cyprus, Aden, Borneo and elsewhere, as erstwhile colonies sought their independence. Those units involved in such activities were mostly armoured cars and scout cars, but on some occasions tanks were deployed. Indeed, it was the norm for British armoured regiments to serve tours in the armoured reconnaissance role, the lighter AFVs being more suitable for aid to the civil power and counter-insurgency operations.

Such disturbances also occurred on the Indian subcontinent, as both Hindus and Muslims sought self-government. Then on August 14, 1947, India and Pakistan became separate countries. This momentous event was sadly accompanied by widespread communal violence, which inevitably led to war between the two new nations – first of all over Kashmir in November 1947, then over the Rann of Kutch in January 1957.

The United Nations mediated and a ceasefire was effected, but not before a number of major tank battles had taken place, in which the Indian-manned, British-built Centurions took on and beat the more sophisticated American-built Pakistani M48 Pattons. In 1965 during the 22-day war, the largest tank battle ever fought in Asia took place, with over 1,500 tanks involved and many being knocked out. On January 10, 1966, the two countries signed an uneasy truce, but in 1971, the Awami League declared East Pakistan to be the independent republic of Bangladesh. This led to Pakistan attacking India from West Pakistan in the "Lightning War". India retaliated by sending some eight divisions, including over 700 tanks (more than 400 Soviet-built T-55s and 300 home-produced Vickers Vijayanta, plus a number of Centurions, French-built AMX-13s and

BELOW: **An Indian Commanding Officer issues orders to his squadron commanders on the eve of battle, April 13, 1948. The Stuart Light Tank behind them is now on a plinth at the Indian War Museum.**

Russian amphibious PT-76s), forcing the Pakistanis into a humiliating surrender. Since then no major conflicts have occurred and both countries now have their own main battle tanks under construction (with outside assistance).

Iran–Iraq

The Iran–Iraq conflict is often forgotten despite being one of the longest-running wars of the 20th century. On September 22, 1980, Saddam Hussein attacked Iran, anticipating a short three-week Blitzkrieg-type campaign, leading to victory using more than 3,000 mainly Soviet-built tanks. Instead the war lasted for eight years and resulted in over a million casualties. Western arms dealers were only too happy to supply both sides with weapons, especially Iran, whose tanks were in a parlous state after years of neglect following the deposing of the Shah, who had taken a great interest in all things military.

Russo–Afghan War

In December 1979, the USSR attempted to take over Afghanistan, invading it with more than 100,000 troops supported by large numbers of tanks, helicopters and jet fighters. For the next ten years they fought a bitter, bloody war against the Mujahedin, who were clandestinely aided by Western finance. Eventually the Soviets realized that they could not win and signed a peace agreement in April 1988, withdrawing troops in 1989. Fighting has continued there ever since, but with different protagonists.

The Balkans

Closer to Europe, the Balkans has been a potential and actual battleground throughout the 20th century. During his lifetime, Marshal Tito managed to hold the various ethnic components of Yugoslavia together – an explosive mixture of Serbs, Croats and Slovenes – and fought successfully against the Germans in World War II. However, following his death the situation deteriorated, with widespread ethnic violence, leading to UN intervention in which British and American main battle tanks were employed in peace-keeping operations.

Sadly, this handful of examples is only the tip of the iceberg, as shown only too often by the twisted hulks of burnt-out tanks found all over the world.

ABOVE LEFT: **Indo-Pakistan conflict. This Pakistani M48 Medium Tank was knocked out by Indian Centurions during the war in 1965.** ABOVE: **Some Indian tank commanders pose with one of their victorious Centurions.** BELOW: **Soviet tanks on the streets of Bratislava in 1968. A stone-throwing youth uses the leading Soviet T-62 to provide cover from the other Russian tanks in this failed uprising, August 1968.** BOTTOM: **War in the Falklands. A small number of British tanks were used in the Falklands War in 1982. Here a Scimitar CVR(t) gains extra protection by being dug in.**

The Arab-Israeli wars

It is ironic that after World War II the dashing image of the *Panzerwaffe* should have been taken over by Jewish tank commanders – the people the Nazis most reviled. The Israeli Armoured Corps was born in battle from small beginnings, yet rapidly became one of the most formidable armoured forces the world has known. Their commanders learned the hard way – on the battlefield – at all levels, putting lessons into practice immediately, instituting a rigorous system of discipline, yet without stifling individual initiative. The resulting potent mixture enabled them time and again to overcome the far larger, better-equipped forces of their Arab neighbours.

During the initial War of Independence in 1948, they had to organize effective armoured units while at the same time obtaining tanks from all over the world. Their first (and only) armoured brigade contained just one tank battalion comprising one company of smuggled in French Hotchkiss Light Tanks, manned by Russian immigrants who spoke little Yiddish, and one company of two Cromwells and one Sherman (stolen from the British), manned by British and South African volunteers. Nevertheless, they performed miracles.

1956 saw another upsurge in violence following the nationalization of the Suez Canal and the decision by Britain and France to send in troops to maintain free, open transit

TOP: **Patton tanks of Israel Defence Force (IDF) 7th Armoured Brigade breaking into Khan Younis on the morning of June 5, 1967, when the Six Day War began.** ABOVE: **Yom Kippur. Israeli Patton tanks advancing across the desert in central Sinai, making for the Suez Canal.**

through the canal. British Centurion tanks landed and took Port Said, but the major armoured effort came from two Israeli armoured brigades – part of their invasion force from Sinai. The Israeli 7th Armoured Brigade, for example, reached the Suez Canal in less than 100 hours, having travelled 241km/150 miles and having fought several fierce battles on the way.

A period of hasty reorganization followed, in which a number of new armoured brigades were formed, and in 1960 the Israelis took delivery of British Centurions, which soon proved their worth against Syrian tanks in border skirmishes. They were followed by more modern tanks, such as American M48A2 Pattons, fortunately in time for the Six Day War of 1967,

LEFT: **Paratroopers with armoured support (Sherman M4A1 Horizontal Volute Spring Suspension with 76mm/2.99in gun and wet stowage) break through to the American colony, north-west of the Old City wall of Jerusalem.**
BELOW: **An excellent photograph of two Israeli Centurions churning through the sands of Sinai during the lightning campaign that lasted just six days.**

"The outcome of the war will depend on our performance ...
If we fail the outcome will be disastrous for the whole campaign ...
There will be heavy fire and the Egyptians will fight well,
so keep moving ... fire from as far as possible, knocking
out enemy tanks and anti-tank guns at long range."
General Israel Tal, then Director of the Israeli Armoured Corps
to his tank commanders

ABOVE: **Part of a company of Merkava MBT in a Palestinian camp. The Israelis are probably the most experienced army in the world as far as street fighting is concerned.**

in which the Israeli armour did particularly well, the individual tank gunnery skills of their tank crews completely dominating their Egyptian and Syrian opponents.

Then followed the War of Yom Kippur in October 1973, when the Egyptians took the initiative, launching a surprise attack across the Suez Canal. The Bar Lev Line was heavily attacked by 280,000 troops and 2,000 tanks, and many defending Israeli tanks were knocked out by man-portable, Soviet-made "Sagger" guided missiles. By the morning of October 8, the Egyptian Army had achieved a tremendous success and had put five divisions across the Canal. Nevertheless, despite being taken by surprise, the Israeli

reservists were soon rushing to join their units, two armoured divisions reaching Sinai during the night of October 7–8. Instead of the expected Egyptian breakout, there followed a period when they merely held their positions and knocked out many of the counter-attacking Israeli tanks. Clearly the Israelis needed to regain the initiative, and so they decided to re-cross the Canal and infiltrate their armour behind the Egyptian lines. After some delay, this was achieved at dawn on October 15, and by October 19 they had the best part of three tank divisions across. They were soon threatening Port Tewfik and the Gulf of Suez, encircling the Egyptians and forcing them into a ceasefire by October 24. Success on the Golan against the Syrians soon followed.

Since then there has been much activity but no all-out war, although Israeli armour, in particular their remarkable Merkava tank (one of many home-grown armoured successes) has been in constant action along their disputed frontiers with the Palestinians. The Israelis have certainly become experts in the difficult art of urban warfare, using heavy armour effectively against short-range urban targets. This requires specialized ammunition for the main armament and the use of the tank's excellent target-acquisition capability coupled with on-board machine-guns to deal with snipers and other threats. Another highly successful weapon on the latest Merkava Mk IV is the remotely activated, internally mounted Soltam 60mm/2.36in mortar which is used most effectively against tank-hunting parties.

Improvements in basic characteristics

Following World War II, while the speed and quantity of tank-building worldwide has slowed down, there are still plenty of new tanks being built, with some new countries indulging in first-time manufacture or in the improvement of less modern tanks so that they are capable of holding their own in future battles. All three of the basic characteristics have seen improvements, as have many other, less vital features.

Regarding firepower, Main Battle Tanks (MBTs) now mount main guns of 120–122mm/4.72–4.80in calibre. However, the fitting of conventional rifled guns has been overtaken by smooth-bore weapons of similar calibre, the only exception among the latest MBTs being the British CR2. Both have a similar range of anti-armour projectiles, which now include fin-stabilized, long rod, DU (Depleted Uranium) penetrators. These are necessary to defeat new forms of armour like the British Chobham – the latest type being called "Dorchester",

which gives a significant increase in protection against both KE (Kinetic Energy) and CE (Chemical Energy) attack. In 1988 the USA announced a new version on the M1A1 with steel-encased depleted uranium armour, two and a half times the density of steel.

Gun performance has also been significantly improved by a wide variety of new vision and gun-laying devices designed to improve the chances of a first-round hit by day or night. For example, some of the fire-control equipment found in the US Army Abrams M1A1 MBT includes a laser rangefinder, a full solution solid-state digital computer and a stabilized day/thermal night sight. The stabilizer allows for accurate firing on the move, the gunner merely placing the reticule in his sight on to the target and using his laser rangefinder to measure the range. The computer then works out and applies the weapon sight offset angles necessary to hit the target, and the gunner

LEFT AND ABOVE: **In these two photographs taken inside the Challenger building plants at what was the Royal Ordnance Factory, Leeds (now closed), tank turrets are being fitted with Chobham armour for increased protection. Compare them with the normal Chieftain turrets alongside.**

opens fire. The gun has a muzzle reference system to measure any bend in the gun tube, while other sensors check wind speed, barrel temperature, ammunition temperature, etc, and automatically feed the results into the computer.

Added protection is afforded to many MBTs by the external fitting of reactive armour in the form of explosive-filled tiles. These detonate and explode outwards when struck by a shaped-charge projectile, thus disrupting the armour-piercing jet and negating its penetrative effect. Internally, sliding armoured doors and armour-protected boxes isolate crew members from on-board ammunition explosions, while automatic fire extinguishing systems will react to a fire and extinguish it.

Engines are now invariably run on diesel or are kerosene-based and despite being smaller in size are more powerful, having to deal with an MBT normally weighing between 60–70 tons. They are also generally simpler to maintain, the Abrams power pack (a Lycoming Textron AGT 1500 gas turbine), for example, being capable of removal and replacement in less than one hour (compared with four hours for the M60 series). Equally, modern-day suspensions give a smoother ride, not only benefiting the crew, but also making the weapon stabilization system more effective.

In addition to all these major new items, there are land-navigation and battlefield information systems, and better day/night viewing devices together with longer-range yet more compact radios. The inevitable result of all these improvements, however, has been a considerable increase in manufacturing costs. Thus, there has been a significant consolidation and specialization within the armaments industry, for example in the UK, first the acquisition of Vickers Defence Systems by Alvis plc in late 2002, and then the take-over of Alvis Vickers by BAe Systems. Building MBTs is clearly an expensive business.

ABOVE LEFT: **Even "bombing-up" a tank on the ranges and not under battlefield conditions is still a time-consuming job. Here crewmen load practice ammunition (note the colour is different from service rounds). In the photograph there are APDS (Armour-Piercing Discarding Sabot) and HESH (High-Explosive Squash-Head) practice rounds, plus bag charges, vent tubes (in the small can he is holding) and belts of machine-gun ammunition for the coaxial machine-gun.**
ABOVE: **Modern tank ammunition includes Armour-Piercing Fin-Stabilized Discarding Sabot rounds such as these for a British 120mm/4.72in tank gun. The part that does the damage is the Long Rod Penetrator (two versions are on show here) to defeat Depleted Uranium armour.** BELOW: **Amphibious light tanks are still extremely useful for reconnaissance purposes. Here a number of Soviet PT-76s swim ashore during a training exercise.**

Training expedients

ABOVE: **Gunnery training simulators were essential to save both expensive training areas and equally expensive track mileage. This Classroom Armament Instructional Mounting for a Chieftain was used by the REME (Royal Electrical and Mechanical Engineers) to instruct gun-fitters.**

Immediately post-World War II, armoured training on both sides of the Iron Curtain was intensified at all levels, with major exercises being held by NATO and Warsaw Pact forces at varying levels of realism. However, it soon became clear that other cheaper and more sustainable methods of training had to be found if vast training damage bills were to be avoided – not to mention the wear and tear on AFVs. Nevertheless, tank crews still had to be kept at the right level of readiness so that they could go to war at a moment's notice.

Considerable work was therefore done on improving indoor static-training devices such as Classroom Simulators, especially for both tank driver/commander and tank gunner/loader/commander skills. While this could not entirely replace actual hands-on training in the AFV, it certainly could and did give all crew members good, basic training and made it easier to sustain follow-on training in regiments, so that tank crews could be kept at a suitable level of operational readiness. In military schools such as the Armor School at Fort Knox, USA, and the RAC (Royal Armoured Corps) Centre (now called the Armour Centre) in the UK and in training regiments, suites of

such training devices have been installed and are used extensively. In addition, it was realized that training a tank driver did not require an AFV with a vastly expensive fighting compartment (i.e. a turret), so now MBTs such as CR2 have a specially built turret-less Driver Trainer Tank (DTT).

Regular gunnery training periods on open ranges are still essential if crews are to become accustomed to live firing. However, the increased range and lethality of tank gun ammunition has made it necessary to invent new training rounds which have similar characteristics to service ammunition, but without the same range or lethality.

Another perennial problem for training at lower levels has been finding a suitable method of registering hits on two-sided exercises. Initially this could only be done by means of on-the-spot umpires, but this not only required manpower, but was in many cases ineffective. There are now training devices that can be fitted to tanks, anti-tank guns/missile launchers, and even to individual personal weapons, which give a realistic impression

FAR LEFT: **The "business end" of an early driver-training simulator. This shows the TV camera on a Link Miles Driving Simulator which was moved on a gantry across a terrain model.**
LEFT: **Instructor's console for the Link Miles Driving Simulator. Note the replica driving controls below the TV screen and the map of the terrain model above them.**

both to the firer and at the target end. When an accurate hit by a suitable type of armour-piercing round is registered on the target vehicle, coloured smoke may be emitted, a siren sounded, or the vehicle engine or gun control computer may be shut down by means of suitably located detectors on board. However, this must be carefully controlled so that the "knocked-out" tank and its crew are not put at risk. The firer also gets a suitable reaction, even as far as reducing the amount of his on-board ammunition, so that in due course he must replenish if he is to continue to take part in the battle.

Restrictions on space in Europe have led to the British seeking training areas further afield. None has been more successful than the British Army Training Unit, Suffield (BATUS), in Alberta, Canada. Armoured units stationed in the UK and Germany now regularly train at BATUS against "live" enemy. In addition, the lowering of the Iron Curtain and the dismantling of the Berlin Wall has led to NATO and erstwhile Warsaw Pact armies exchanging training grounds and working together to deal with common problems.

Additionally, the mere fact that much of the equipment on a modern tank is computer-controlled means that built-in training devices are commonplace, allowing crews to practise their drills without even having to leave the tank hangar.

ABOVE: **Bale out! With a coloured smoke pyrotechnic belching smoke (for 30 seconds) denoting a "kill", the crew of this Chieftain bale out of their "knocked-out" tank.** BELOW: **Fording water obstacles is another part of tank training. Note the tall "conning tower" fixed to the commander's hatch of this Chieftain and the rubber sealing covers to prevent water from getting inside the tank.**

Wars in Iraq

In early August 1990, tiny oil-rich Kuwait was invaded by its neighbour Iraq, which boasted the fourth largest and supposedly most powerful army in the world. The Iraqis used thousands of Russian-built T-series tanks (such as T-62 and T-72 MBT) to spearhead their invasion in typical Blitzkrieg style. Fortunately, apart from a few "prophets of doom", Saddam Hussein found few allies, while the United Nations, with America leading the way, imposed an immediate naval blockade. This was swiftly followed by an impressive build-up of sea, land and air forces in Saudi Arabia, to back up the UN resolution ordering Iraq to withdraw. Operation "Desert Shield", as it was called, was followed by Operation "Desert Storm" in which first Coalition air forces and then ground troops were employed. The ground offensive, Operation "Desert Sabre", was launched on February 23, 1991. Meticulously planned and executed with élan, its speed and direction came as a complete surprise to the Iraqis. With armour to the fore – in particular the main battle tank playing a major role – it was yet another example of a highly successful all-arms team action. It was also fought on a 24-hour battlefield day, in which the vastly superior night-fighting capability of the British Challenger and the American Abrams tanks was in evidence from the outset.

The battle went so quickly that many observers could not believe what they saw on their television screens all over the world. Thousands of the enemy were killed, wounded or captured – out of all proportion to the small numbers of Coalition casualties. The much-vaunted Soviet tanks were a disaster, and in many cases dug in so deeply that they could not traverse their turrets, while their AFV batteries had been removed and used to light underground shelters rather than work their vehicle electrical systems! The fourth largest army in the world turned out to be a paper tiger thanks to the sheer professionalism of the Allied tank crews. Pentagon officials estimated that some 4,000 Iraqi tanks were destroyed in the 100-hour battle, which ended on February 28 when the Coalition forces cut the highway from Kuwait to Basra, thus preventing the bulk of the battered and defeated Iraqi Army from escaping.

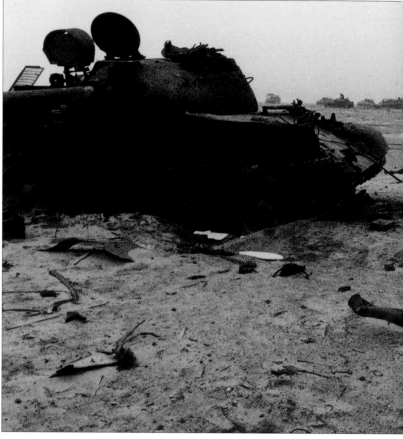

ABOVE LEFT: **Operation "Desert Storm". Crews of British Challenger 1s carry out last-minute adjustments before going into battle.** ABOVE: **The detritus of war. In the foreground are the knocked-out blackened hulks of two Iraqi tanks during the aftermath of Operation "Desert Storm", barely recognizable as once combat-ready MBTs. A convoy of Coalition force vehicles can be seen in the background.** BELOW: **A British Challenger 1 advances to meet the enemy.**

The second Gulf War

World opinion prevented the Coalition forces from "finishing the job" and calling Saddam Hussein to account. Instead, for the next 14 years they vacillated, while Iraq threatened its neighbours with supposed "Weapons of Mass Destruction" and the Iraqi leader continued to oppress his own people. Eventually the Allies once again decided to act, although this time world opinion was not as solidly behind

BELOW: **Operation "Telic". Striking picture of the "business end" of a 2nd Royal Tank Regiment Challenger 2. Note the 7th Armoured Brigade "Desert Rat".** BOTTOM: **Gunner action! A CR2 belonging to the 2 RTR Battlegroup traverses on to a target.**

the USA and UK as it had been on the first occasion. Nevertheless, on March 20, 2003, the Allied armies invaded Iraq from Kuwait, the British elements targeting the southern city of Basra, while the Americans drove all-out for Baghdad. The success of the armour-led Allied columns was even more spectacular than in 1991, the war-fighting being over in a matter of just a few days. Once again the American and British main battle tanks had shown their complete

superiority – a testament to how effective tanks still are on the modern battlefield, provided they are manned by thoroughly professional, properly motivated, well-disciplined and well-trained tank crews. Operation "Iraqi Freedom", as it was known by the Americans, and Operation "Telic", as it was called by the British, showed once again that it is the all-arms team that wins battles and that the human element in the shape of the tank crew is still the most important ingredient.

The future

As must be evident from what has been covered already, the tank undoubtedly played a major part in securing victory in both World Wars and has gone on to prove itself time and time again ever since, being employed in most of the high-intensity conflicts that have occurred worldwide. There was also a large armoured presence on both sides of the Iron Curtain ready to take part in World War III if the unthinkable had ever happened and the world had descended into nuclear war. This led to increasingly large numbers of sophisticated Main Battle Tanks (MBTs) being built by both sides before the thaw in the Cold War started.

There is now, however, no doubt that things are changing, principally because the end of the Cold War has seen a downsizing of most European armies, leading to considerable over-capacity in tank-building and associated armaments industries, despite the continuing lucrative trade in the upgrading and modernization of older MBTs. However, this has not been the case worldwide where countries in the Far East, such as China, Japan and the Republic of Korea, now have their own tank-building industries, some even exporting to neighbours and further afield. In the West there has thus been a declining MBT market, especially as a number of countries, including the USA and UK, have started to favour a more balanced force composition. Therefore, as well as needing a "heavy" element based upon MBTs, infantry fighting vehicles and Self-Propelled (SP) artillery, they have now stated a requirement for a "light" element that can be air-transportable

TOP: **One of the obvious employments for British armour will be in peacekeeping operations on behalf of NATO and the UN, as in Kosovo. The photograph shows three elements of IFOR, including a Challenger 2 MBT and a CVR Scimitar Light Tank.** ABOVE: **Fitting old tanks with more powerful guns, power packs, etc, is now big business all over the world. Here an American-built M48 has been fitted with a more powerful diesel engine – the AVDS 1790 2C tank engine – by means of installing a TCM/GPD simplified dieselization kit.**

in medium-range transport aircraft, such as the C-130 Hercules. This challenges the armaments industry to produce a class of tank weighing about 16 tons – a very demanding requirement for any would-be manufacturer who must produce a new tank with firepower, protection and mobility on a par with the current 70-ton MBT, but weighing some 75 per cent less. This calls for considerable innovation, and consideration is now being given to lighter, smaller, wheeled AFVs as well as tracked vehicles. Miniaturization of components and the use of machinery to perform crew tasks (such as automatic loaders) so as to cut down on the space requirements also becomes a major issue.

LEFT: Added protection against HEAT (High-Explosive Anti-Tank) projectiles is achieved by the fitting of tiles of Explosive Reactive Armour (ERA), as on this Russian T-72 tank. BELOW: Testing new materials for the future. An early test model, developed in 2000 by the Defence Evaluation and Research Agency (DERA) in partnership with Vickers Defence Systems, to examine the trend towards smaller, lighter MBTs. It has a plastic/glass fibre composite hull rather than one made of conventional steel. It was known as the Advanced Composite Armoured Vehicle Platform (ACAVP), but christened by some the "Tupperware Tank"! Its basic purpose was for stress and strain analysis under field conditions.

In addition, the use of non-conventional, lighter, composite armour is also being studied. An example of such lighter systems is the much-debated American "Future Combat System". It is early days yet and, at least for the time being, MBTs will continue to rule.

Various MBTs and other AFVs are now being offered with a variety of alternative subsystems – such as varying power packs, fire-control systems and night/day vision devices – to suit all customers' needs. As mentioned before, the British CR2 is now the only top-grade MBT with a rifled gun. This could possibly change as consideration is currently being given to replacing it by one of a number of similar calibre smoothbore guns. New types of ammunition specifically for urban warfare have been developed, such as the American Multi-Purpose Anti-Tank round (MPAT) to create breaches in buildings for assault team access and the Israeli Anti-Personnel Anti-Material tank round (APAM) containing six sub-munitions with thousands of tungsten cubes for controlled fragmentation.

Suffice it to say that for the time being anyway, there is little chance of the MBT going out of fashion or being replaced by some other weapon system such as the armed helicopter. Although the balance of the "Firepower, Protection and Mobility" equation may alter and thus produce a more varied selection of the weapon system that we call the "Tank", their future place on the battlefield as an indispensable member of the battle-winning all-arms team still appears secure.

ABOVE: On guard at the edge of Podujevo during Operation "Agricola". A close-up of the CR2 belonging to the Commanding Officer of 2 RTR, 7th Armoured Brigade (note the "Desert Rat" emblem). LEFT: After many years without an armaments industry, Japan, like other Far Eastern countries, now makes its own tanks. These are Type 61 MBTs, the first home-produced tank since World War II.

A–Z of Modern Tanks

1945 to the Present Day

The Cold War and the limited wars in such places as the Far and Middle East have ensured the continuing need for tanks. In particular, there has been a requirement for Main Battle Tanks (MBTs) with improved, more powerful weapons, sophisticated gun control and viewing equipment, more effective protection, and better engines and running gear. MBTs have grown larger and heavier, yet are faster and more manoeuvrable, with tanks like the Abrams and Challenger being far superior to their World War II equivalents. Major changes have also occurred among tank builders. In the last war it was really only the USA, USSR, Germany and the UK that produced tanks. Now there are some 30 nations either building their own MBT, a "cloned" replica of a major producer's tank, or an upgraded version of an older model. China is now a major producer, as are, once again, Germany and France. Even smaller nations like Israel and Japan build excellent MBTs. With the advent of global terrorism, there has also been a shift in requirement away from MBTs towards more strategically mobile AFVs, but mounting larger weapon systems than in the past.

LEFT: **Vastly superior to Leopard 1, the Leopard 2 is currently one of the best Main Battle Tanks in service in the world.**

A41 Centurion Medium Tank

The A41 Centurion is undoubtedly one of the major British successes in tank design and production. The mock-up was ready in May 1944, but troop trials did not begin until May 1945 (due to a Government ruling banning development work on all projects that could not be in service by 1944), so it never saw action during World War II. Twenty pilot models were ordered mounting a 17pdr gun as their main weapon and with a mixture of Polsten cannon (in a ball-mount) or Besa machine-gun as secondary armament, the first ten only having Polstens. The Mark II (A41A) incorporated numerous improvements including a cast turret, commander's vision cupola and a combined gunner's periscope and coaxial Besa machine-gun. This became the first production model, known thereafter as the Centurion 2.

Over 4,400 Centurions in 12 different models were produced, the most plentiful being over 2,800 Centurion 3s. This version incorporated numerous major improvements, including the more efficient 484.7kW/650bhp Rolls-Royce Meteor engine, the Ordnance Quick-Firing 20pdr main gun together and new gun control equipment. It was the first British tank that could fire accurately on the move thanks to its gyroscopic gun control system, while the policy of not storing ammunition above the turret ring greatly increased its chances of survival by limiting ammunition fires. Many other modifications and improvements were constantly being added as the years went by, the most important being the fitting of the 105mm/4.13in rifled gun. Centurions saw action in Korea,

TOP: **An early Centurion Mark 3 on the test track at the Fighting Vehicle Research and Development Establishment, Chertsey. Originally armed with a 17pdr, then 20pdr and finally 105mm/4.13in gun, the Centurion was one of Britain's most successful post-war main battle tanks and sold in large numbers worldwide.** ABOVE: **Sweden made an initial order for 88 Mark 3s (known as the Stridsvagn 81). Later they would purchase more, including Centurion Mark 10s (known as Stridsvagn 102), as seen here.**

Vietnam and numerous other wars, having been purchased by many nations, perhaps most notably by the Israelis who had over 1,000 Centurions in service at one time. At the beginning of the 21st century this excellent AFV is still to be found in use with some countries.

RIGHT: **Sweden purchased two Marks of Centurion in the late 1950s, renaming them Stridsvagn 101 and 102. This is an up-armoured version of the Stridsvagn 102.** BELOW RIGHT: **The Israeli Army was at one time the largest user of the Centurion, with over 1,000 in service. This one is on show at the IDF Tank Museum at Latrun. Initially the Centurion had a poor reputation until General Israel Tal, a man of wide technical expertise and character, took a hand and instilled the essential gunnery discipline into his crews which swiftly showed the gun's inherent accuracy.** BOTTOM: **A Centurion Beach Armoured Recovery Vehicle, whose primary role was to rescue drowned vehicles to the shoreline and to keep exits from landing craft clear during beach landings. They went on serving in the British Army long after other Centurions, one each being manned by the Royal Marines on HMS** *Fearless* **and HMS** *Intrepid* **(Landing Platform Dock Ships).**

In addition to gun tanks, there are Centurion Armoured Recovery Vehicles (ARVs), specialized Beach ARVs, Assault Engineer – Armoured Vehicle Royal Engineers (AVRE) and armoured bridgelayers – Armoured Vehicle Launched Bridge (AVLB).

In 2004 there were four major countries with significant numbers of Centurion gun tanks/variants in service, although Israel has converted most of its 1,000 to other roles. Jordan had 293 (called *Tariq*), which are now being replaced by Challenger 1 Main Battle Tanks. Singapore had between 12 and 63, based in Brunei and Taiwan. South Africa had 224, which are known as *Olifant*.

A41 Centurion Medium Tank

Entered service: 1945
Crew: 4
Weight: 43,182kg/42.5 tons
Dimensions: Length – 7.47m/24ft 6in
Height (over turret hatch) – 3.02m/9ft 11in
Width – 3.40m/11ft 2in
Armament: Main – 17pdr (76mm/2.99in) gun
Secondary – 7.92mm/0.312in Besa machine-gun
Armour: Maximum – 101.6mm/4in
Powerplant: Meteor V12 petrol, 484.7kW/650hp
Performance: Speed – 35.4kph/22mph
Range – 193.1km/120 miles

M1A1/M1A2 Abrams Main Battle Tank

The M1A1/2 Abrams Main Battle Tank is the prime weapon of the US armoured forces, and is manufactured by General Dynamics Land Systems. The first M1 tank came into service in 1978, the M1A1 in 1985, and the M1A2 in 1986. Since then, system enhancement packages have kept this AFV as a state-of-the-art weapons system, and undoubtedly one of the most formidable tanks in the world.

Built using steel-encased depleted uranium armour to protect against modern HEAT (High-Explosive Anti-Tank) weapons, the M1A1's main weapon is the 120mm/4.72in M256 smoothbore gun (the original M1 had a 105mm/4.13in gun), developed by Rheinmetall GmbH of Germany, with a 7.62mm/ 0.3in M240 machine-gun mounted coaxially on its right. The commander also has a 12.7mm/0.5in Browning M2 machine-gun and the loader a 7.62mm/0.3in M240 machine-gun.

Needless to say, the tank is crammed full of the most advanced electronic equipment. The commander's station is equipped with an independent stabilized day and night vision

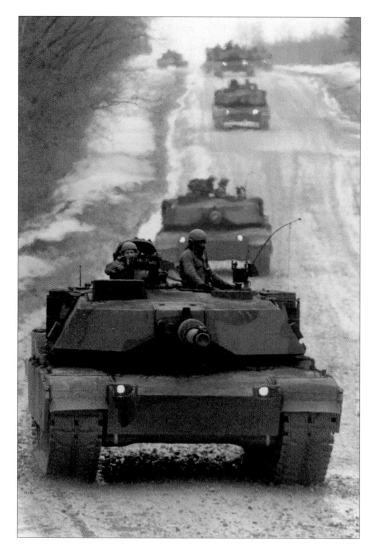

TOP: **The XM1 tank programme was begun in 1971, and five years later Chrysler was awarded a three-year contract to produce 11 pilot vehicles and spares at the Detroit Arsenal Tank Plant. In 1982, Chrysler sold its tank building subsidiary to General Motors. First-production MBT was completed in February 1980. It is anticipated that in total (up to and including the M1A2 MBT upgrades), the US Army will order over 1,000 such M1 upgrades, while sales to other countries (e.g. 555 to Egypt) were agreed and delivered in 1998. This photograph of a basic M1 gives a good impression of its power, speed and protection.** RIGHT: **A column of Abrams returning from training. With a combat weight of 57,154kg/56.3 tons and a maximum road speed of 67.6kph/42mph, the Abrams is a formidable sight to meet anywhere.**

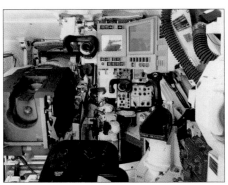

LEFT: **Three of the four-man crew are visible in this photograph of an M1A1, two of the turret crew manning secondary armament (both 7.62mm/0.3in machine-guns), while the driver's excellent central position is evident.** BELOW: **Excellent internal view of the M1A1 turret, looking at the gunner's station and the rear of the breech.**

device with a 360-degree view, automatic sector scanning, automatic target cueing of the gunner's sight and back-up fire control. The gunner's specially modified seat also locks him in position so that even on the move his eyes are unwaveringly locked in his sight.

The powerplant was originally diesel for the M1/M1A1 models, but the M1A2 is fitted with a new gas turbine engine which is more powerful but uses more fuel. However, like all of the most modern tanks, the Abrams is built in a modular fashion, whereby new feature "suites" or packages can replace any previous one. In this way, any of the main features of the tank – turret, armament, and power pack – can be constantly refined and upgraded.

The Abrams combat effectiveness has been proved in the recent conflicts in the Gulf, where it dominated the battlefield completely. It has also been sold to Egypt, Saudi Arabia, Kuwait and Australia. Those M1A1s in service with the USMC are fitted with a Deep Water Fording Kit (DWFK).

BELOW: **Three Abrams use the concrete test slopes at the factory to show off their paces. The MBT can deal with a 60 per cent gradient, a side slope of 30 per cent and a 0.914m/3ft vertical obstacle.** BOTTOM: **Operation "Desert Storm". Abrams manoeuvre in the Iraqi desert during Operation "Desert Storm", when the US Army had 1,956 M1A1 Abrams MBTs deployed with units in Saudi Arabia.**

M1A1 Abrams MBT

Entered service: 1985
Crew: 4
Weight: 57,154kg/56.3 tons
Dimensions: Length – 9.77m/32ft 0.5in
Height (over turret hatch) – 2.44m/8ft
Width – 3.66m/12ft
Armament: Main – 120mm/4.72in M256
smoothbore gun
Secondary – 1 x 7.62mm/0.3in coaxial machine-gun,
plus 1 x 12.7mm/0.5in machine-gun (commander)
and 1 x 7.62mm/0.3in machine-gun (loader)
Armour: Thickness unknown, depleted uranium,
steel
Powerplant: AGT 1500 gas turbine,
1,118.6kW/1,500hp
Performance: Speed – 67.6kph/42mph
Range – 465.1km/289 miles

AAI Rapid Deployment Force Light Tank

Manufactured by the AAI Corporation in conjunction with the US Army's Tank-Automotive Research and Development Command Armored Combat Vehicle Technology (ACVT), the AAI AFV was an air-portable light tank designed to boost the firepower of Rapid Deployment Forces (RDFs). This tank was a development of the HSTV(L) project and was part of the continuing attempt to perfect air-transportable firepower

that began during World War II and is especially relevant to the war scenarios of today. The vehicle shares its main armament with the earlier AAI HSTV(L) – the ARES 75mm/2.95in hypervelocity automatic gun, with a range of over 12.1km/7.5 miles at maximum elevation. This weapon was so advanced that the ARES Corporation was forbidden by the US Government to sell it to anyone other than NATO member countries. The

prohibition effectively killed off the AAI RDF, although the company did try to rescue the vehicle by bringing out a heavier model mounting a 76mm/2.99in main gun in a newly designed turret. However, there was no sales interest generated and in 1985 the project was shelved.

AAI RDF Light Tank	

Entered service: 1983 (prototypes only)
Crew: 3
Weight: 13,200kg/13 tons
Dimensions: Length – 7.34m/24ft
    Height (over turret hatch) – 2.24m/7ft 4in
    Width – 2.54m/8ft 4in
Armament: Main – 75mm/2.95in ARES
    or 76mm/2.99in M32 gun
    Secondary – 7.62mm/0.3in machine-gun
Armour: Maximum – Unrevealed
Powerplant: General Motors 6V53T 6-cylinder
    diesel, 224kW/300hp
Performance: Speed – 64kph/39.9mph
    Range – 500km/310.6 miles

ABOVE AND LEFT: **Two views of the AAI Corporation's Rapid Deployment Force Light Tank (RDF/LT) which mounted the ARES Corporation 75mm/2.95in hypervelocity automatic gun with a range of some 12.1km/7.5 miles! Based upon an experimental AFV, it had export problems due to its experimental main armament. This meant it could not be exported outside NATO, so a 76mm/2.99in gun was offered as an alternative.**

Alan Degman Main Battle Tank

First revealed in the late 1990s, the Croatian Degman MBT traces its origins back to the Yugoslavian M-84A, itself a Russian T-72 derivative manufactured in Yugoslavia since the previous decade. Specifications for this vehicle are sketchy, but it is based closely upon its predecessor and weighs approximately 40,600kg/40 tons, and is powered by a new diesel engine with automatic transmission delivering a top speed of around 60kph/37mph with a range of about 600km/370 miles. The turret is of a new Croatian design and manufacture, and includes the fitting of ERA (Explosive Reactive Armour) modules that are formed in distinctive long bands and are also positioned on the glacis plate and sides skirts. (Most Eastern European and ex-Soviet satellite states have been influenced by the Russian predilection for ERA.)

It mounts the up-rated D-81 125mm/4.92in smoothbore main gun, served by an automatic loader, thereby allowing a crew of just three, along with two machine-guns – one coaxial 7.62mm/0.3in and the other of 12.7mm/0.5in for anti-aircraft and close-quarter defence.

The vehicle's fire control is based on the Omega system designed and manufactured in Slovenia, and its communications systems have been sourced from the UK.

Other enhancements include NBC (Nuclear, Biological and Chemical) protection, navigation and safety systems. The Degman is currently in service with the Croatian Army and has also been sold to Kuwait. There are also command, ARV (Armoured Recovery Vehicle) and engineering variants.

Alan Degman MBT

Entered service: 1999
Crew: 3
Weight: Approximately 40,600kg/40 tons
Dimensions: Close to T-72 specifications
Armament: Main – 125mm/4.92in D-81 gun
Secondary – 1 x 7.62mm/0.3in and
1 x 12.7mm/0.5in machine-guns
Armour: Unspecified
Powerplant: Unspecified diesel generating around
745.7kW/1,000hp
Performance: Speed – Approximately 60kph/37mph
Range – Approximately 600km/370 miles

LEFT AND BELOW: **The RH Alan Degman Croatian MBT that was first seen in 1999 is an enhanced version of the Yugoslavian T-84A MBT, which in turn was based on the Russian T-72 MBT. Although sometimes called the M95, it is very similar to the M-84/M-84A and is armed with a 125mm/4.92in smoothbore gun with an automatic loader.**

Alvis Scimitar Combat Vehicle Reconnaissance (Tracked)

LEFT: **The latest version of the original Alvis Combat Vehicle Reconnaissance Scimitar is the Alvis Sabre Reconnaissance Vehicle, which has the same original chassis as the Scimitar, but with the two-man operated Fox turret, mounting the L94 Hughes 7.62mm/0.3in chain gun and extra bins.**
BELOW: **A CVR(T) Scimitar on training. 165 rounds were carried (in clips of three) for the 30mm/1.18in Rarden cannon. Basically a single-shot weapon, it could fire short bursts of up to six rounds.**
BOTTOM LEFT: **A trio of Scimitars on training/ operations in the north of the NATO area.**

The Scimitar is the light reconnaissance version of the Combat Vehicle Reconnaissance (Tracked) – CVR(T) – series produced by Alvis of Coventry. It was primarily designed to deal with hostile Armoured Personnel Carriers (APCs) and other lightly armoured vehicles at ranges of about 1,000m/1,087yds or more, and also for close reconnaissance and internal security roles.

Like the Scorpion, its outstanding cross-country performance and low silhouette, combined with its small size, enabled the Scimitar to perform these tasks very well indeed. It was also ideal for the "shoot and scoot" tactics of fighting a delaying battle. The vehicle's hull and turret was built out of a newly developed aluminium-zinc-magnesium alloy and mounts a 30mm/ 1.18in Rarden gun as its main armament, along with a coaxial 7.62mm/0.3in machine-gun. Powered by a Jaguar XK J60, 4.2-litre 6-cylinder engine giving a top speed of 80.5kph/50mph, the Scimitar has a crew of three, with the driver in the hull and the other two in the turret side by side – each with a cupola.

A later 1993 upgrade of the Scimitar was the Sabre, equipped with a new turret, mounting the L49 Hughes 7.62mm/0.3in high velocity chain gun along with a Rarden 30mm/1.18in cannon. As with all the vehicles in this successful series, the Scimitar was sold abroad to various countries.

Alvis Scimitar CVR(T)

Entered service: 1973
Crew: 3
Weight: 7,900kg/7.8 tons
Dimensions: Length – 4.39m/14ft 4.5in
　Height (over turret hatch) – 2.09m/6ft 10.5in
　Width – 2.18m/7ft 2in
Armament: Main – 30mm/1.18in Rarden cannon
　Secondary – 7.62mm/0.03in machine-gun
Armour: Unspecified
Powerplant: Jaguar 4.2 litre petrol, 141.7kW/190hp
Performance: Speed – 80.5kph/50mph
　Range – 644km/400 miles

LEFT: **One of the latest versions of this replacement for the ubiquitous Saladin armoured car was this Scorpion 90, which Alvis fitted with a 90mm/3.54in Cockerill Mark 3 gun, reducing its ammunition load from 40 rounds with the 76mm/ 2.99in to 34 with the 90mm/3.54in. Malaysia bought some 26 Scorpion 90s in the late 1980s and early 90s, as did Nigeria (33), and it is also believed that Venezuela bought an undisclosed number in the 1980s (possibly over 80).**

BELOW: **The first prototype appeared in 1969 (production three years later) and has been in service in various forms ever since as the lead AFV of the Combat Vehicle Reconnaissance (Tracked) family. Used in both low and high intensity warfare, Scorpion mounts a 76mm/ 2.99in gun and has a crew of three.**

Alvis Scorpion Combat Vehicle Reconnaissance (Tracked)

Produced by Alvis of Coventry as a replacement for the ageing Saladin and Saracen wheeled vehicles, the Combat Vehicle Reconnaissance (Tracked) – CVR(T) – family comprised: Scorpion – Fire Support; Scimitar – Anti-APC (Armoured Personnel Carrier); Spartan – APC; Samson – ARV; Striker – Anti-Tank Guided Weapon (ATGW); Sultan – ACV (Armoured Combat Vehicle); and Samaritan – Ambulance.

All were deliberately compact enough to be air-transportable. The Scorpion, with its light but strong aluminium alloy armour weighed 7,800kg/7.67 tons and was fast, with a top speed of 80.5kph/

50mph. It had the same basic design, layout and crew numbers as the Scimitar, but was fitted with a more powerful main gun – the L23A1 76mm/2.99in – along with a coaxial 7.62mm/0.3in machine-gun.

The L23A1 fires four types of ammunition: HESH (High-Explosive Squash-Head) – capable of defeating medium armour at a range of up to 3,500m/11,500ft and also very effective against the tracks and side armour of most MBTs; HE (High-Explosive); Smoke – base ejection type; and Canister – a short-range anti-infantry round which produces 800 steel pellets to devastating

effect. The gun has a maximum range of 5,000m/16,400ft and a relatively low muzzle velocity which contributes to the accuracy by producing a light recoil and low barrel wear (each barrel can fire 3,000 HESH rounds). One of the latest versions is Scorpion 90, which is equipped with the 90mm/3.54in Cockerill Mark 3 main gun.

LEFT: **Cutaway drawing of a Scorpion CVR(T), fitted with its flotation screen. It was built of aluminium alloy armour, which did produce some problems; however, it was certainly both light and fast. The original version is no longer in British Army service. However, as the other photographs show, a variety of other models are still available.**

Alvis Scorpion CVR(T)

Entered service: 1973
Crew: 3
Weight: 7,800kg/7.67 tons
Dimensions: Length – 4.39m/14ft 5in
   Height (over turret hatch) – 2.08m/6ft 10in
   Width – 2.18m/7ft 2in
Armament: Main – 76mm/2.99in or 90mm/ 3.54in gun
   Secondary – 7.62mm/0.03in machine-gun
Armour: Maximum – Unspecified thickness, aluminium
Powerplant: Jaguar 4.2 petrol, 141.7kW/190hp
Performance: Speed – 80.5kph/50mph
   Range – 644km/400 miles

AMX-13 Light Tank

Designed just after World War II, the AMX-13 (the "13" in its name is its original designated weight in tonnes) was initially manufactured in 1950 by Atelier de Construction Roanne, then from the early 1960s by Mecanique Creusot-Loire, and finally by GIAT into the late 1980s, a lengthy period that saw it grow into a large family of successful variants.

The AMX-13 was manned by a crew of three and powered by a SOFAM 8-cylinder petrol engine, giving it a top speed of 60kph/37.3mph and a range of 400km/248.5 miles. Its most distinctive feature was the extraordinary rear-mounted, low-profile, oscillating turret.

Initially mounting a long-barrelled 75mm/2.95in self-loading main gun based on a pre-1945 German design, it was then upgraded to a 90mm/3.54in weapon and then in 1987 Creusot-Loire introduced a 105mm/4.13in low-recoil gun option. When the AMX-13 was sold abroad, some other countries also mounted their own weapons of choice.

All these main gun upgrades continued to be based on the original oscillating turret, which proved to be troublesome. The excellent tough chassis remained essentially the same, though there were changes of engine from petrol to diesel. Variants included an

ABOVE: **The highly successful AMX-13, designed soon after the end of World War II by Atelier de Construction d'Issy les Moulineaux, the significance of the "13" being its original weight in tonnes. Production was subsequently moved to the Creusot-Loire factory at Chalon sur Saone, and over 7,700 AFVs were eventually built, including variants such as self-propelled artillery guns, anti-aircraft guns and infantry fighting vehicles. One feature of the original model was its oscillating FL-10 turret, containing a 75mm/2.95in gun and coaxial machine-gun.**

armoured personnel carrier, a light recovery vehicle, an armoured bridgelayer, different calibres of self-propelled gun and an artillery rocket-system launch platform. Regular upgrade packages extended the AMX-13's service life, and almost 8,000 vehicles were manufactured.

ABOVE: **Now on show at the Israeli Tank Museum at Latrun, Israel purchased a number of AMX-13s from France in 1956 and used them in the Six Day War. However, the gun, with its two revolver-type magazines (each 6 rounds), was ineffective against the front armour of Soviet-sourced tanks such as T-54/T-55, so it was phased out and sold elsewhere.**

AMX-13 Light Tank

Entered service: 1950
Crew: 3
Weight: 15,000kg/14.8 tons
Dimensions: Length – 4.88m/16ft
    Height (over turret hatch) – 2.3m/7ft 6.5in
    Width – 2.51m/8ft 3in
Armament: Main – 75mm/2.95in or 90mm/3.54in
    or 105mm/4.13in
    Secondary – 2 x 7.5mm/0.295in or 7.62mm/0.3in
    machine-guns
Armour: Maximum – 25mm/0.98in
Powerplant: SOFAM 8Gxb petrol, 186.4kW/250hp
Performance: Speed – 60kph/37.3mph
    Range – 400km/248.5 miles

AMX-30 Main Battle Tank

Manufactured by Giat Industries, the AMX-30 Main Battle Tank was first produced in the mid-1960s as a lighter yet more powerfully armed replacement for the American-supplied M47. It had a crew of four and mounted one 105mm/4.13in main gun with a coaxial 20mm/0.79in cannon and a 7.62mm/0.3in machine-gun. It was powered by a Hispano-Suiza 12-cylinder multi-fuel engine that gave it a top speed of 65kph/40.4mph and a range of 450km/280 miles.

The AMX-30 B2 was an improved version of the AMX-30, some of them newly made and some with the B2 upgrade packages retrofitted to earlier models. The upgrade included an automatic fire-control system and NBC (Nuclear, Biological and Chemical warfare) proofing, enabling the AMX-30 to fight in a contaminated atmosphere. Over 3,500 of this vehicle were built, including variants such as self-propelled howitzers, anti-aircraft missile or gun systems and armoured recovery vehicles.

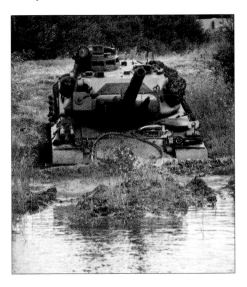

TOP: **Good photograph of an AMX-30 in a Paris street. Like AMX-13 and others, the AMX-30 was designed post-war to replace the American M47s which had been supplied by the USA via the Mutual Defence Aid Programme.** ABOVE: **The AMX-30 D armoured recovery vehicle has a dozer blade mounted at the front of the hull, plus two winches and a hydraulic crane.** LEFT: **Most advanced of the AMX-30 models is the AMX-30 B2, which was the one in main French Army service. It incorporated many of the improvements, such as laser rangefinder, low-light TV and an integrated fire-control system. There is even an AMX-30 "Stealth" MBT fitted with radar-absorbing material and carefully shaped to reduce the radar signature.**

AMX-30 MBT

Entered service: 1967
Crew: 4
Weight: 36,000kg/35.43 tons
Dimensions: Length – 9.48m/31ft 1in
  Height (over turret hatch) – 2.29m/7ft 6in
  Width – 3.1m/10ft 2in
Armament: Main – 105mm/4.13in smoothbore gun
  Secondary – 1 x 20mm/0.79in cannon and
  1 x 7.62mm/0.3in machine-gun
Armour: Maximum – 80mm/3.15in
Powerplant: Hispano-Suiza HS 110 multi-fuel,
  522kW/700hp (for AMX-30 B2)
Performance: Speed – 65kph/40.4mph
  Range – 450km/280 miles

AMX–32 Main Battle Tank

The AMX-32 was developed in 1975 as an export model of the AMX-30 and was available with either a 105mm/4.12in rifled main gun or a 120mm/4.72in smoothbore alternative, along with a coaxial 20mm/0.79in cannon and a 7.62mm/0.3in anti-aircraft machine-gun. The layout, weight, armour and crew numbers remained the same as its predecessor, but the engine was upgraded to the more recent Hispano-Suiza 110-S2R supercharged model developing 800hp, coupled with the ENC gearbox, with lock-up torque converter and hydrostatic steering. However, when no sales interest was generated, the project was dropped in favour of the AMX-40.

TOP: **The AMX-32 was the export model of the AMX-30, having a redesigned turret and thicker front hull armour to give better armoured protection. Weighing just over 38 tons and mounting a 120mm/4.72in smoothbore (second prototype) gun, it was much more powerful than the AMX-30, but had a marginally worse performance.** ABOVE: **Good side view of the AMX-32 export model.** BELOW LEFT: **Despite the improvements, including an all-welded turret in the second prototype, no purchasers materialized, and the AMX-32 was withdrawn.**

AMX-32 MBT

Entered service: 1979
Crew: 4
Weight: 39,000kg/38.38 tons
Dimensions: Length – 9.48m/31ft 1in
　　　　　Height (over turret hatch) – 2.29m/7ft 6in
　　　　　Width – 3.24m/10ft 7in
Armament: Main – 120mm/4.74in gun
　　　　　Secondary – 1 x 20mm/0.79in cannon and
　　　　　1 x 7.62mm/0.3in machine-gun
Armour: Maximum – 80mm/3.15in
Powerplant: Hispano-Suiza HS 110-S2R,
　　　　　596.6kW/800hp
Performance: Speed – 65kph/40.4mph
　　　　　Range – 530km/329 miles

AMX-40 Main Battle Tank

In the early 1980s came the next in the Giat manufactured, export-driven AMX series. As the AMX-32 had failed to attract any sales, the company decided to produce yet another upgrade, the AMX-40. This vehicle was based on the earlier AMX-32, with its essential design and layout remaining much the same, including the main 120mm/4.72in smoothbore main gun and the COTAC fire-control system.

The main improvements came in armour and mobility, the armour thickness being increased, especially on the frontal arc. A new engine was also installed, the Poyaud 12-cylinder diesel, with a top speed of 70kph/43.5mph and a range of 530km/329 miles. In order for the vehicle to make use of this additional power, an extra road wheel was added to each side, and wider tracks were fitted to reduce ground pressure and increase traction, all of which improved the overall performance of the vehicle.

Brought out in 1983, and despite three prototypes completed by late 1984, there was insufficient sales interest in the AMX-40, so it was withdrawn.

AMX-40 MBT	
Entered service: 1983	
Crew: 4	
Weight: 43,700kg/43 tons	
Dimensions: Length – 10m/32ft 9.5in	
Height (over turret hatch) – 2.29m/7ft 6in	
Width – 3.3m/10ft 10in	
Armament: Main – 120mm/4.72in gun	
Secondary – 1 x 20mm/0.79in cannon and	
1 x 7.62mm/0.3in machine-gun	
Armour: Maximum – 100mm/4in	
Powerplant: Poyaud V12X diesel, 820.3kW/1,100hp	
Performance: Speed – 70kph/43.5mph	
Range – 530km/329 miles	

LEFT: **At 54,000kg/53.1 tons, with a 120mm/ 4.72in smoothbore gun and a speed in excess of 65kph/40.4mph, the Italian Ariete is a formidable second-generation MBT and well able to hold its own on the modern battlefield. Its Oto Breda 120mm/4.72in smoothbore gun can engage targets both by day and night, while it has a laser warning system for added protection (electrically operated smoke grenades being automatically launched when the MBT is lazed by the enemy).**

Ariete Main Battle Tank

The 1995 Consorzio Iveco Fiat and Oto Melara produced C1 Ariete, which is the latest Italian main battle tank. Weighing 54,000kg/53.1 tons and with a crew of four, it is powered by a Fiat V12 MTCA turbo-charged, 12-cylinder diesel engine, giving it a top speed in excess of 65kph/40.4mph and a range of 550km/342 miles. The turret, with crew of commander, gunner and loader, mounts the Oto Breda 120mm/4.72in

smoothbore main gun and is also armed with a 7.62mm/0.3in machine-gun mounted coaxially and another 7.62mm/ 0.3in machine-gun fitted on the roof for air defence. The vehicle carries the latest optical and digital-imaging and fire-control systems, enabling it to fight day and night and to fire on the move. The tank is built in a modular fashion so that elements such as the power pack can be replaced swiftly and easily.

Ariete MBT	

Entered service: 1988
Crew: 4
Weight: 54,000kg/53.1 tons
Dimensions: Length – 7.59m/24ft 11in
   Height (over turret hatch) – 2.5m/8ft 2in
   Width – 3.60m/11ft 9.5in
Armament: Main – 120mm/4.72in gun
   Secondary – 2 x 7.62mm/0.3in machine-guns
Armour: Unspecified
Powerplant: IVECO V12 MTCA diesel,
   970kW/1,300hp
Performance: Speed – 65kph/40.4mph
   Range – 550km/341.8 miles

Arjun Main Battle Tank

The Arjun Mark 1 is India's first indigenous main battle tank, designed to replace the Vickers Vijayanta. This project began in 1974 as an attempt at armour autonomy but production was delayed by various problems, and the Arjun was held up for many years before finally entering service

at prototype stage in 1987. Built using composite armour, the vehicle is manned by a crew of four (commander, loader and gunner in the turret, and driver in the hull) and mounts a 120mm/4.72in stabilized main gun and also a 7.62mm/ 0.3in machine-gun in its turret, along with all the necessary modern additions

of stabilization, digital fire control, optical and laser sighting and fire suppression. Powered by a MTU MB 838 Ka 501 water-cooled diesel engine delivering a top speed of 72kph/44.7mph and equipped with hydro-pneumatic suspension, the Arjun has a range of approximately 400km/248.5 miles.

LEFT: **In 1974, the Indian Combat Research and Development Establishment began work on a successor to the ageing Vijayanta. However, it was not until April 1987 that its successor, the Arjun, was unveiled. The new MBT has a crew of four and mounts a 120mm/4.72in rifled gun. It is anticipated that some 125 MBTs will be produced in "slow time" for "home" consumption.**

Arjun MBT	

Entered service: 1987 (prototype)
Crew: 4
Weight: 58,000kg/57.1 tons
Dimensions: Length – 9.8m/32ft 2in
   Height (over turret hatch) – 2.43m/8ft
   Width – 3.17m/10ft 5in
Armament: Main – 120mm/4.72in gun
   Secondary – 1 x 12.7mm/0.5in and
   1 x 7.62mm/0.3in machine-guns
Armour: Unspecified
Powerplant: MTU MB 838 Ka 501 diesel,
   1,045kW/1,400hp
Performance: Speed – 72kph/44.7mph
   Range – 400km/248.5 miles

ASCOD 105 Light Tank

The ASCOD 105 Light Tank emerged in 1996, built as a private commercial venture by a consortium of Spanish and Austrian companies, Santa Barbara Sistemas of Spain and Styr-Daimler-Puch of Austria, who manufactured the vehicle between them and also purchased some of its parts internationally.

Known as the "Ulan" in Austria and in Spain as the "Pizarro", the ASCOD 105 is a light tank variant of the APC ASCOD already being built by the Austrian part of the consortium, Styr-Daimler-Puch. The tank uses the chassis of its sister vehicle, which can carry up to eight infantrymen in addition to the crew of three. The main difference between the two is in the turret and its main armament – the ASCOD 105 being fitted with South

African Denel turret, mounting a 105mm/4.13in GT7 main gun. Weighing 28,500kg/28 tons and fitted with torsion bar suspension, the ASCOD 105 is powered by a German MTU 8VTE22 V90 diesel engine, giving it a top speed of 70kph/43mph and a range of 500km/310 miles.

Alternative main armament mounts include a two-man South African Rooikat turret with a 20mm/0.79in Mauser cannon, an Italian turret fitted with a 25mm/0.98in cannon and two TOW ATGW (Tube-launched, Optically-tracked, Wire-guided Anti-Tank Guided Weapon) launchers and a lower, flatter American turret with just an externally mounted 105mm/4.13in main weapon that reduced the vehicle's profile considerably.

All turret configurations feature digital fire control, gun stabilization, as well as the latest night-vision, navigation and safety systems. As well as being deployed by both Austrian and Spanish armoured forces, the vehicle has also been sold to Thailand.

ASCOD 105 Light Tank	

Entered service: 1996
Crew: 4
Weight: 28,500kg/28 tons
Dimensions: Length – 6.61m/21ft 8in
   Height (over turret hatch) – 2.76m/9ft 0.5in
   Width – 3.15m/10ft 4in
Armament: Main – 105mm/4.13in GT7 gun
   Secondary – 2 x 7.62mm/0.3in machine-guns
Armour: Unspecified
Powerplant: MTU 8V183TE22 V90 diesel, 447.4kW/600hp
Performance: Speed – 70kph/43.5mph
   Range – 500km/310.7 miles

LEFT: **Developed in the early 1950s, this Soviet tank destroyer was designed for use with Red Army airborne forces. It mounted a 57mm/2.24in light assault gun on a T-70 light tank chassis. Now obsolete, the photograph shows the twin LAA version the ZSU-57-2 LAA gun, which was introduced in 1957.**

ASU-57 TD

Entered service: 1957
Crew: 3
Weight: 7,400kg/7.3 tons
Dimensions: Length – 3.73/12ft 3in
    Height (over turret hatch) – 1.42m/4ft 8in
    Width – 2.2m/7ft 2.5in
Armament: Main – 57mm/2.24in gun
    Secondary – 1 x 7.62mm/0.3in machine-gun
Armour: Maximum – 15mm/0.59in
Powerplant: ZIL-123 6-cylinder petrol, delivering
    82kW/110hp
Performance: Speed – 65kph/40.4mph
    Range – 320km/198.8 miles

ASU-57 Tank Destroyer

The ASU-57 was part of the USSR's attempt to develop air-portable firepower for use by airborne forces in the years of the Cold War, entering service in 1957. Weighing 7,400kg/ 7.3 tons and manned by a crew of three, it mounted a 57mm/2.24in CH-51M gun around which the superstructure was built, which was set back and sloped to the front where the gun protruded. It also mounted a 7.62mm/0.3in machine-gun for anti-aircraft and close-quarter defence. Powered by a ZIL-123 6-cylinder petrol engine, the ASU-57 had a top speed of 65kph/40.4mph and a range of 320km/198.8 miles. The ASU-57 was used by Soviet forces and their satellite client states well into the 1980s, at which time it would have been beyond the capability of its gun to knock out the then current NATO MBTs, so it was used for other purposes such as LAA (light anti-aircraft).

ASU-85 Tank Destroyer

The ASU-85 was a continuation of the ASU series, emerging in 1962 and based upon a PT-76 chassis, though not required to be amphibious but rather air-portable. The main changes from the ASU-57 approach were to the superstructure, which was now completely enclosed, and in its armament, which was upgraded to an 85mm/3.35in D-70 gun in a fixed mount along with a coaxial 7.62mm/0.3in SGMT machine-gun and cupola-mounted 12.7mm/0.5in anti-aircraft machine-gun. At more than double the weight of its predecessor, the ASU-85 now required a new engine, and was fitted with a V6 diesel engine, giving it a speed of 45kph/28mph and a range of 260km/ 161 miles.

ASU-85 TD

Entered service: 1962
Crew: 4
Weight: 15,500kg/15.26 tons
Dimensions: Length – 6m/19ft 8in
    Height (over turret hatch) – 2.1m/6ft 10.5in
    Width – 2.8m/9ft 2in
Armament: Main – 85mm/3.35in D-70 gun
    Secondary – 1 x 12.7mm/0.5in and
    1 x 7.62mm/0.3in machine-guns
Armour: Maximum – 40mm/1.58in
Powerplant: V6 diesel, 179kW/240hp
Performance: Speed – 45kph/28mph
    Range – 260km/161.5 miles

LEFT: **Introduced in 1962, with an all-up weight of 15,500kg/15.26 tons, the ASU-85 was the logical successor to the ASU-57 and mounted an 85mm/ 3.35in gun.**

LEFT: The US Army provided Brazil with a number of their M41 Light Tanks, which the Brazilians took into service and improved. For example, their M41B had its old petrol engine replaced by a 302kW/450hp diesel, while the M41C (seen here) had better vision equipment, additional armour plate and a new 90mm/3.54in gun.

Bernardini M41 Light Tank

Bernardini M41C Light Tank

Entered service: 1983
Crew: 4
Weight: 25,000kg/24.6 tons
Dimensions: Length – 8.21m/26ft 11in
    Height (over turret hatch) – 2.76m/9ft 0.5in
    Width – 3.2m/10ft 6in
Armament: Main – 90mm/3.54in gun
    Secondary – 1 x 12.7mm/0.5in and
    1 x 7.62mm/0.3in machine-guns
Armour: Unspecified
Powerplant: Scania DS14 diesel, 302kW/450hp
Performance: Speed – 70kph/43.5mph
    Range – 600km/372.8 miles

A clever choice or sales pitch determined a useful future for the US-made M41 Walker Bulldog. After an upgrade package which combined items shopped for on the open market and indigenously produced parts which were then assembled locally, the Brazilian Government equipped their armoured forces with an AFV well suited for their requirements. The first drawback was the short operational range of the original M41 petrol engine. This was soon identified and quickly dealt with by replacement using a locally built Scania DS14 diesel engine, along with new cooling and electrical systems. The original 76mm/2.99in gun was also upgraded by being re-bored locally to 90mm/3.54in, and the final upgrade, the M41C, had additional armour and improved vision equipment. By March 1985, 386 M41s had been upgraded.

Bernardini X1A1 and X1A2 Light Tanks

The Bernardini X1A1 was another example of tank recycling for the US, who was able to sell on "obsolete" tanks, and helped Brazil in the development of their own armaments industry. It was based on the M3A1 Stuart Light Tank, combined with another indigenously put together upgrade package consisting of a new locally designed and built turret which mounted a French-bought 90mm/3.54in main gun.

This model, however, did not progress beyond the prototype stage and was followed by the X1A2, which had a completely redesigned chassis fitted with a new two-man turret in which to mount the 90mm/3.54in main gun. The X1A2 model that was accepted by the Brazilian Army weighed almost 19 tons, with its Saab-Scania 6-cylinder 224kW/300hp diesel engine giving it a top speed of 55kph/34mph and a range of 600km/372.8 miles.

LEFT: **The Bernardini X1A2 Light Tank. Essentially its predecessor had been an upgraded US M3A1 Stuart Light Tank fitted with a locally produced 90mm/3.54in French gun. In due course it was replaced by the 100 per cent Brazilian-made X1A2 seen here, which had a brand-new two-man turret and 90mm/3.54in gun. This came into service in the Brazilian Army, but its successor, the X1A3, did not.**

Bernardini X1A2 Light Tank

Entered service: 1978
Crew: 3
Weight: 19,000kg/18.7 tons
Dimensions: Length – 6.5m/21ft 4in
    Height (over turret hatch) – 2.45m/8ft 0.5in
    Width – 2.6m/8ft 6.5in
Armament: Main – 90mm/3.54in gun
    Secondary – 1 x 12.7mm/0.5in and
    1 x 7.62mm/0.3in machine-guns
Armour: Unspecified
Powerplant: Saab-Scania DS11 diesel,
    224kW/300hp
Performance: Speed – 55kph/34.2mph
    Range – 600km/372.8 miles

Challenger 1 Main Battle Tank

Manufactured by Vickers Defence Systems (VDS), the Challenger 1 is the last in the progression of British MBTs tracing their origin back to the Centurion through Chieftain. It is based on the Shir 2 – originally an updated Chieftain variant, designed as an export project for the Shah of Iran's armed forces, but accepted by the British Army under the re-designation "Challenger". Built using advanced Chobam composite armour and cast and rolled steel, the emphasis is on protection and firepower rather than mobility. The CR1 mounts a Royal Ordnance 120mm/4.72in L11A5 rifled main gun, fitted with

ABOVE: **Operation "Desert Storm". A CR1 moves up into position. Note the additional armour plates on its sides and fuel drums on its rear.** BELOW LEFT: **The "Chinese Eye" on the side of the turret denotes that this CR1 belongs to 1 RTR.**

a thermal sleeve, fume extractor and muzzle brake, and has two 7.62mm/0.3in machine-guns, one coaxial with the main gun. These weapons are operated by a three-man turret crew – commander, gunner and loader, with the aid of the latest digital and optical range-finding and fire-control equipment. It is powered by a Rolls-Royce CV12 engine, giving it a top speed of 57kph/35mph and a range of 450km/280 miles. Three different models of the CR1 have been developed, with upgrade suites fitted to ensure pre-eminence as one of the world's most formidable tanks.

In September 1978, the MOD had placed an order with the ROF Leeds to supply 243 Challenger 1s. Four years later, in December 1982, the MBT was accepted by the General Staff, by which time production was well under way. The first order was sufficient to equip four armoured regiments, and in July 1984 there was a further order for 64 more to equip a fifth regiment. In 1986, ROF Leeds was bought by Vickers Defence Systems and a new factory was built at Leeds, identical to the VDS Newcastle works. The new factory was operational by late 1987, when a further order for another 76 CR1s was placed by MOD. The last of the CR1s was delivered in mid-1990. Ten years later the last CR1 was phased out of British Army service (late 2000), being replaced by Challenger 2 MBT. Then in March

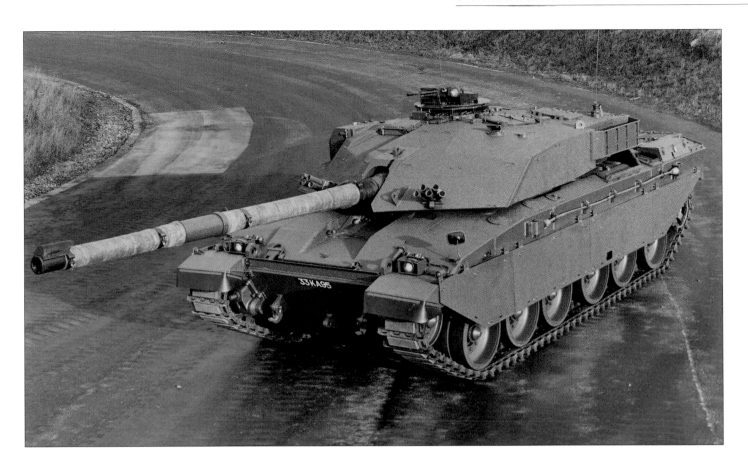

1999 it was agreed that 288 CR1s would be supplied to Jordan (renamed Al Hussein in Jordanian service).

In addition to the MBTs, the following variants were built: 17 Challenger Training Tanks and 30 Challenger Armoured Repair and Recovery Vehicles (CR ARRV).

The CR1 demonstrated its battle-winning capabilities with a highly successful combat record in the first Gulf War. It was heavily involved in Operation "Desert Storm", destroying some 300 Iraqi MBTs for the loss of no Challengers.

ABOVE AND BELOW: **Factory fresh. These remarkably crisp photographs were taken on "Roll-out" Day at ROF Leeds before it closed. They give excellent all-round views of CR1 No. 33KA 95.** BOTTOM LEFT: **This CR1 is part of IFOR on operational service in the Balkans.**

Challenger 1 MBT

Entered service: 1982
Crew: 4
Weight: 62,000kg/61.02 tons
Dimensions: Length – 8.33m/26ft 4in
   Height (over turret hatch) – 2.5m/8ft 2.5in
   Width – 3.52m/11ft 6.5in
Armament: Main – 120mm/4.72in L11A5 gun
   Secondary – 2 x 7.62mm/0.3in machine-guns
Armour: Unspecified
Powerplant: Rolls-Royce CV12 diesel,
   894.8kW/1,200bhp
Performance: Speed – 57kph/35.4mph
   Range – 450km/279.6 miles

Challenger 2 Main Battle Tank

TOP AND ABOVE: **The British Army's latest MBT, Challenger 2 (CR2) is now battle-proven, having seen active service both in the Balkans and the Gulf War. As can be seen from these two photographs taken on training, the turret incorporates second-generation Chobham armour – known as "Dorchester", which gives significantly improved protection against both Kinetic and Chemical Energy attacks.**

A logical development of the Vickers-built Challenger 1, the Challenger 2 shares its predecessor's hull and automotive parts but has many new and improved features, making it a vastly improved MBT. These include Chobham second-generation composite armour, an NBC (Nuclear, Biological and Chemical) protection suite, and, for the first time in any British tank, both a heating and a cooling system in the crew compartment.

The vehicle's armament consists of a gyrostabilized Royal Ordnance 120mm/4.72in rifled main gun designated the L30, along with a coaxial McDonnell Douglas Helicopter Systems 7.62mm/0.3in chain gun and a 7.62mm/0.3in anti-aircraft machine-gun. Its fire-control system is the latest generation in digital computer technology, as are its range-finding, sighting and fire-suppression systems.

The CR2 carries a crew of four. Power is supplied by a Rolls-Royce Perkins Condor CV12 894.8kW/1,200bhp engine and it is equipped with a Hydrogas variable spring suspension system.

The initial order placed by the MOD in June 1991 was for 127 CR2 MBTs, plus 13 Driver Training Tanks. First to be completed were the Driver Training Tanks (in 1993), so that training could commence before the gun tanks began to arrive.

Interestingly, CR2 was the first post-World War II British tank to be designed, developed and produced by a single manufacturer, VDS (now Alvis Vickers – part of BAe Systems). The first CR2 MBTs were formally accepted into service on May 16, 1994.

Two months later, VDS were awarded a second contract to supply a further 259 CR2 MBTs and nine Training Tanks, together with the necessary training and logistic support. This was sufficient to maintain a total of six CR2 MBT-equipped armoured regiments each of 36 CR2s, of which the Royal Scots Dragoon Guards were the first to be so equipped in June 2000. Of course, events have moved on since then, and

RIGHT, BELOW RIGHT AND BOTTOM: **Three views of Britain's Challenger 2 Main Battle Tank on training and operations. This was originally a private venture begun in the 1980s by Vickers Defence Systems and eventually led to a firm production proposal in 1988. The MOD approved the building of nine prototypes (seven at Leeds and two at Newcastle), which led to a contract being awarded for 127 CR2s, plus 13 Driver Training Tanks. CR2 was the very first British Army tank to be completely developed by a single contractor, VDS (now Alvis Vickers – part of BAe Systems). The tank did exceptionally well in Operation "Telic" (the war in Iraq), being rated as one of the best MBTs in the world, along with Abrams, Merkava and Leopard 2.**

the CR2-equipped 7th Armoured Brigade has taken part in war fighting in Iraq, proving the excellence of both the MBT and its crewmen to the world. Sadly, its reward appears to have been a "restructuring" that will reduce the number of CR2s in front-line service. Presumably the rest will be "mothballed". It was at the end of February 2002 that the British Army took delivery of the last of its CR2s, the total being 386.

To date, there has been only one export success, namely to Oman. Their first order, placed in July 1993, was for 18 CR2s, four CR ARRVs and two Driver Training Tanks. This was followed in November 1997 by a further order for 20 CR2 MBTs, again for Oman.

Challenger 2E Main Battle Tank

In the early 1990s, VDS (now Alvis Vickers) embarked on the development of an enhanced export model of the CR2 MBT. It ran for the first time in 1994 and since that date has completed many trials in temperate and desert conditions. The aim has been to take it as the manufacturers have stated: "a generation ahead of current in service MBTs". Undoubtedly CR2 has proved itself to be a "Top Gun" among the world's leading MBTs.

Challenger 2 MBT	
Entered service: 1994	
Crew: 4	
Weight: 62,500kg/61.51 tons	
Dimensions: Length – 8.33m/27ft 4in	
Height (over turret hatch) – 2.49m/8ft 2in	
Width – 3.52m/11ft 6.5in	
Armament: Main – 120mm/4.72in L30A1 gun	
Secondary – 1 x 7.62mm/0.3in L94A1 chain gun	
and 1 x 7.62/0.3in L37A2 machine-gun	
Armour: Unspecified	
Powerplant: Perkins CV12 TCA Condor diesel, 894.8kW/1,200hp	
Performance: Speed – 60kph/37.3mph	
Range – 450km/279.6 miles	

Chieftain Main Battle Tank (FV 4202)

Britain's successor to their world-beating Centurion was originally designed in 1956 by Leyland Motors, Centurion's "design parents", who built three prototypes. Then in 1961–62, six more were completed and trials took place. The following year the tank was taken into British Army service and production continued at ROF Leeds and Vickers Defence Systems, Newcastle.

The first true British Main Battle Tank (Centurion was strictly a medium gun tank), the Chieftain had a somewhat chequered early career due to problems with its engine (cracking of cylinder liners, failure of lip seals and piston ring breakages), which meant that it had to be continually up-rated from 436.3kW/585bhp (Mark 4A), to 484.7kW/650bhp (Mark 5A), then to 536.9kW/720bhp (Mark 7A) and finally to 559.3kW/

TOP: **Chieftain on training. There were a total of 12 different Marks of Chieftain, the last (Mark 12) being a Mark 5 with IFCS, Stillbrew armour, TOGS and the No. 11 NBC system.** ABOVE: **A Chieftain MBT moves across the RAC Centre training area during the yearly "Open Day" that used to be held at Gallows Hill, north of Bovington – but sadly no longer.**

750bhp (Mark 8A). Designed as a multi-fuel engine, it was normally run on diesel and as such was extremely dirty. It also showed a tell-tale smoke plume when starting up, which could give away its position. Nevertheless, despite these early problems the Chieftain settled down to become a reliable and well-liked tank.

It was of conventional design with a forward driving compartment, central fighting compartment and a rear compartment for the engine, gearbox and transmission. The driver was centrally positioned in the hull and when closed down adopted a reclining position, which meant that the hull height could be reduced, thus lowering the overall height of the tank's silhouette. In the fighting compartment the loader/radio operator was on the left of the main armament, with the gunner and commander seated on the right. All had the necessary inter-communication equipment and all-round vision devices, both for day and night viewing.

The main armament was the highly effective 120mm/4.72in L11A5 rifled tank gun, which used the bagged charge system for the first time in a British tank, the projectile and charge being separately loaded, the latter being ignited by means of an electrically fired vent tube. This reduced loader fatigue and gave a maximum rate of fire of some eight to ten rounds in the first minute, then six rpm thereafter. Initially the system employed a Ranging machine-gun – a 12.7mm/0.50cal Browning Heavy machine-gun which fired flashing tipped trace ammunition, but this was later replaced by a Tank Laser Sight.

Apart from the Mark 1s, all Chieftains in British Army service were retro-fitted with the fully integrated Improved Fire-Control System (IFCS), which ensured a considerable degree of accurate, first round hits on static targets at up to 3,000m/ 9.843ft and on moving targets at up to 2,000m/6,562ft.

The Marconi Fighting Vehicle Control System gave four modes of control (stabilizer, power traverse, hand and emergency) and allowed targets to be engaged with reasonable accuracy while on the move. Other gunnery equipment included night IR/WL sights (used in conjunction with the IR/WL searchlight mounted on the left-hand side of the turret) and TOGS (Thermal Observation and Gunnery Sight).

The L60 engine was coupled to a TN 12 epicyclic gearbox, incorporating a Merrit-Wilson differential steering system and electrohydraulic gear selection, with six forward and two reverse gears, plus an emergency low reverse. In all, there were 12 Marks of Chieftain, with various armour configurations, including a passive armour package known as Stillbrew. Some 1,350 Chieftains were built, of which 450 were exported.

The Chieftain was phased out of British Army service in 1996, but may still be found in Iran, Iraq, Jordan, Oman and Kuwait (their Chieftains saw combat during the Iraqi invasion in 1990). The Chieftain was also used as a test bed for the Marconi Marksman twin anti-aircraft gun turret and the "Jagd Chieftain" which mounted a 120mm/4.72in gun in its hull, and was also used to develop the Shir 1 (Chieftain 800), Shir 2 (Chieftain 900) and Khalid (FV 4211). Additionally, there were three variants which are still serving in various parts of the world;

• Chieftain ARRV (Armoured Repair and Recovery Vehicle), which is basically a Chieftain ARV fitted with a powerful crane that can lift a complete CR1 power pack.

• Chieftain AVRE (Armoured Vehicle, Royal Engineers) which, unlike the Centurion AVRE, does not mount a 165mm/6.49in demolition gun but can carry out a variety of engineer tasks with its bulldozer blade (removing obstacles), plastic pipe fascines (filling ditches), plus mine-clearing (either with a mine plough fitted or by using its Giant Viper rocket-propelled system) and laying Class 60 trackway.

• Chieftain AVLB (Armoured Vehicle Launched Bridge), that can be fitted with a variety of single span, folding or "scissors-type" bridges.

TOP: **A Chieftain fitted with the Pearson Engineering track width mine plough system (as fitted to some Chieftain AVLBs during Operation "Desert Storm").**
ABOVE: **Chieftain 900, the Royal Ordnance Factory's private venture main battle tank completed in 1982. Its layout was basically the same as the Chieftain, but with the British-developed Chobham armour.** BELOW: **A Chieftain AVRE, carrying pipe fascines and towing a Giant Viper mine clearing rocket device.**

Chieftain Mark 5 MBT (FV 4201)

Entered service: 1963 (Mark 1)
Crew: 4
Weight: 55,000kg/54.13 tons (combat-loaded)
Dimensions: Length (gun forward) – 10.87m/
   35ft 8in
   Width (including searchlight) – 3.66m/12ft
   Height (overall) – 2.89m/12ft
Armament: Main – 120mm/4.72in L11A7 rifled gun
   Secondary – 2 x 7.62mm/0.3in machine-guns,
   one coaxial and one on the commander's cupola
Armour: Not given
Powerplant: Leyland L60 petrol engine (Mark 7A),
   536.9kW/720bhp
Performance: Speed – 48kph/30mph
   Range – 400–500km/250–300 miles

Charioteer Tank Destroyer

The Charioteer was a post-World War II development that gave the Royal Armoured Corps a tank destroyer armed with a 20pdr main gun and replaced the aging A30 Avenger and Archer anti-tank weapons that had been manned by the Royal Artillery. This was achieved without any new vehicle having to be designed and was built using existing resources to fill the gap in requirements until something better could be sourced. A recycled Cromwell chassis was modified to take a new, larger turret mounting the same 20pdr main gun as that of the new Centurion tank. This created a powerful tank destroyer at a low unit cost. With a weight of 28,960kg/28.5 tons and powered by a Rolls-Royce Meteor V12 petrol engine, the Charioteer had a top speed of 50kph/31mph and a range of 266km/165 miles. When compared with the Centurion Main Battle Tank, however, its performance was poor, and after 1958, when the Centurion's main armament was upgraded with the 105mm/41.3in L7 gun, the Charioteer became obsolete.

ABOVE AND LEFT: **The FV 4101 Charioteer Tank Destroyer was a refurbished Cromwell on which was mounted a new, larger turret containing the 20pdr gun that was also fitted to the Centurion. These two photographs are of the Charioteer at the Bovington Tank Museum.**

Charioteer TD	
Entered service: 1954	
Crew: 4	
Weight: 28,960kg/28.5 tons	
Dimensions: Length – 6.43m/21ft 1in	
Height (over turret hatch) – 2.44m/8ft	
Width – 3.05m/10ft	
Armament: Main – 20pdr (83.88mm/3.3in) QF (quick-firing) gun	
Armour: Maximum – 60mm/2.36in	
Powerplant: Rolls-Royce Meteor V12 petrol, 447.4kW/600hp	
Performance: Speed – 50kph/31mph	
Range – 266km/165 miles	

Conqueror Heavy Tank

The appearance of the Russian JS-3 Heavy Tank, with its powerful 122mm/4.8in main gun and thick armour, established the need for heavier British main battle tanks. In 1946 it was therefore decided to produce a completely new range of tanks based on the FV200 Universal Tank, of which the FV201 was the basic gun tank.

Conqueror was developed from the original FV201 prototype, powered by a Rolls-Royce Meteor M120 V12 petrol engine with Merritt-Brown transmission with a modified Horstman suspension. Its main armament, the 120mm/4.72in rifled L1 gun, mounted in a well-shaped turret, was derived from an American tank gun, which in turn was derived from an anti-aircraft gun.

The Conqueror was the first British tank in which the shell case and projectile were separate – and with the Conqueror this was not an advantage because a large brass shell case was used to hold the propellant rather than a bag charge, and this made it very heavy and

ABOVE: **The massive Conqueror Heavy Tank weighed 66,043kg/65 tons. While they were capable of dealing with the heavy Soviet tanks (like JS-3), Conqueror was sadly too large and too heavy, being withdrawn in the mid-1960s when the Centurion 105mm/4.13in gun came into service.**
BELOW LEFT: **The Conqueror Heavy Tank on training.**

cumbersome to load, while the stowage was limited to 35 rounds in the turret. Throughout its career the Conqueror was plagued by various electrical and mechanical malfunctions, and while necessary to combat the threat of the Soviet heavy tanks, it proved difficult and cumbersome to use and was generally unpopular with the crews.

Conqueror Heavy Tank

Entered service: 1956
Crew: 4
Weight: 66,043kg/65 tons
Dimensions: Length – 11.58m/38ft
    Height (over turret hatch) – 3.35m/11ft
    Width – 3.96m/13ft
Armament: Main – 120mm/4.72in L1 gun
    Secondary – 2 x 7.7mm/0.303in machine-guns
Armour: Maximum – 178mm/7.01in
Powerplant: Rover Meteor M120 petrol, 604kW/810hp
Performance: Speed – 34kph/21.1mph
    Range – 153km/95.1 miles

LEFT AND BELOW: **Armed with a powerful 90mm/3.54in limited traverse gun, the Jagdpanzer Kanone was something of a hangover from the highly successful German wartime tank destroyers. One major advantage was that it could fire standard US Army 90mm/3.54in tank gun ammunition. It continued in service for many years, some being modified so as to carry and launch the TOW anti-tank guided missile.**

Jagdpanzer Kanone Tank Destroyer

The Jagdpanzer Kanone was a Cold War tank destroyer based on the Hetzer of World War II. The idea behind these vehicles was to use the defensive capacity of a low-silhouette chassis to mount larger fixed guns with limited traverse and elevation. This concept originated from German tank designers reacting to the desperate events at the end of the World War II when various chassis were used to develop tank destroyers.

Hidden away in barns or buildings, or in prepared hull-down positions, they were very effective in the last-ditch defence of the Nazi regime. The thinking remained essentially the same when faced with the massive forces of the Soviet Eastern Bloc, and so the Jagdpanzer Kanone was built.

It mounted a powerful Rheinmetall 90mm/3.54in limited traverse main gun and two 7.62mm/0.3in machine-guns. Power was provided by a Daimler-Benz 8-cylinder diesel engine, giving it a top speed of 70kph/43.5mph and a range of 400km/248.5 miles. However, no sooner had production been completed than the whole concept of a fixed gun tank

destroyer was brought into question and quickly fell out of fashion. Fortunately for the Jagdpanzer Kanone, its excellent chassis could be easily modified and converted to other uses.

With their guns removed and plated over, they morphed to become the Jagdpanzer Rakete Jaguar 2, mounting TOW (Tube-launched, Optically-tracked, Wire-guided) anti-tank guided missiles. A total of 750 Jagdpanzer Kanones were

built for the Germany Army between 1965 and 1967. Then, in late 1972 the Belgians ordered some 80 improved versions of the tank destroyer, which had the complete Renk transmission, final drives, suspension and tracks of the German Marder Mechanised Infantry Combat Vehicle, and gave it the Belgian Army designation of "JPK-90". None of these tank destroyers are now in front-line service with either army.

Jagdpanzer Rakete Jaguar Tank Destroyer

The Jagdpanzer Rakete Jaguar was developed from the Jagdpanzer Kanone, which it replaced. The first prototype was completed by Hanomag and was followed by a further six, three of which were built by Hanomag and three by Henschel from 1963 onwards.

Four years later the Jagdpanzer Rakete Jaguar had succeeded the Jagdpanzer Kanone in production, 370 being built by the following year, half by each of the manufacturers. The main difference between the two is in the main weapon system mounted, although there were also other modifications to the Jagdpanzer Kanone's chassis, hull and front superstructure in order to mount the new weapon system. This was the European manufactured long-range HOT (*Haute subsonique Optiquement Téléguidée*) anti-tank missile, fired from a single roof-mounted launcher equipped with a thermal sight for nightfighting.

Powered by the same Daimler-Benz 8-cylinder diesel engine, the Rakete Jaguar had the same speed and range as its predecessor. The second version of the Jagdpanzer Rakete was a retrofit to the Jagdpanzer Kanone itself, with its main gun removed and the hole plated over in order to mount the TOW (Tube-launched, Optically-tracked, Wire-guided) missile system.

ABOVE AND BELOW: **The Jaguar replaced the Jagdpanzer Kanone, and is based on its modified chassis, coming into production in the late 1960s. It mounted a long-range anti-tank guided missile, there being two models – Jaguar with the HOT missile and Jaguar 2 with TOW.**

A total of 162 Jagdpanzer Kanones were converted into TOW ATGW (Anti-Tank Guided Weapon) carriers from 1983–85. The system already had its Texas Instruments night sight, while the TOW missile flies faster than HOT but has an almost identical range (3,750m/12,303ft as compared with 4,000m/13,123ft).

Jagdpanzer Rakete Jaguar TD

Entered service: 1967
Crew: 4
Weight: 25,500kg/25.1 tons
Dimensions: Length – 6.77m/22ft 2.5in
   Height (over turret hatch) – 2.16m/7ft 1in
   Width – 2.95m/9ft 8in
Armament: Main – HOT missile launcher
   Secondary – 2 x 7.62mm/0.3in machine-guns
Armour: Maximum – 50mm/1.97in
Powerplant: Daimler-Benz MB837 8-cylinder diesel, 372.9kW/500hp
Performance: Speed – 70kph/43.5mph
   Range – 400km/248.5 miles

ABOVE: **Jagdpanzer Rakete Jaguar, mounting the HOT missile, which has both semi-automatic IR guidance and optical manual guidance, where the commands are transmitted via a wire which is immune to jamming. Missiles largely took over from guns in the post-war anti-tank role.**

Leclerc Main Battle Tank

Stemming from an abandoned Franco-German MBT design project of the 1980s, the Leclerc (named after the World War II Free French liberator of Paris) entered service in 1992 and is the prime weapon of the French armoured forces. Built using welded rolled steel and composite armour, weighing 56,000kg/55.1 tons and fitted with a hydro-pneumatic suspension system, it is powered by a SACM V8X-1500 12-cylinder diesel engine, giving a top speed of 72kph/ 44.7mph and a range of 450km/279.6 miles.

The main armament is a 120mm/4.72in smoothbore gun served by an automatic loader capable of delivering 12 rounds per minute. There is also a 12.7mm/0.5in heavy machine-gun mounted coaxially and a 7.62mm/0.3in machine-gun for anti-aircraft and close quarter defence.

The Leclerc also carries all the latest digital optical, fire-control and battlefield management systems. Giat Industries have designed a new turret for the Leclerc which can accommodate a 140mm/5.51in smoothbore gun together with an automatic loader in the turret bustle, but currently there are no plans to replace the existing gun. There are plans for future improvements that include enhanced command and control systems, battlefield identification friend-or-foe, automatic target-tracking, a defensive aids suite, a new thermal imager and enhanced armour.

Leclerc variants include an ARV (Armoured Recovery Vehicle), an ARV with K2D mine-clearing equipment and an armoured engineer vehicle which is similar to the ARV but can be fitted with specialist engineering equipment (now in prototype stage).

In 2002 the French revealed that they were studying further upgrades to the Leclerc MBT in service with the French Army, aiming for 2015. These are likely to include mobility, lethality, survivability, command and control, communications and intelligence, and support. As far as survivability is concerned, Giat Industries are looking to incorporate several layers of protection, the first line of defence being stealth and the second a soft kill kit. They have built an AMX-30 Stealth demonstrator and are evaluating a version of the stealth kit for the Leclerc. The soft kill kit will probably be based upon

ABOVE: **The Giat Industries MBT – called the Leclerc from 1986 onwards – was first mooted in 1985 and made its first appearance just five years later in 1990 at the Satory defence exhibition. This photograph shows it in the ring at the French Armour School's annual demonstration at Saumur. So far, over 400 have been built and used to equip French tank regiments, while the United Arab Emirates have also purchased 436 tropicalized Leclercs.** LEFT: **A French Army Leclerc on operations in Kosovo.**

ABOVE: **A Close-up of the FINDERS Battle Management System as installed in a Leclerc MBT.**
RIGHT: **A pair of Leclercs on training. The 120mm/4.72in smoothbore gun is the same calibre as that fitted to Leopard 2 and has an automatic loader containing 22 ready-rounds.**

a basic countermeasures kit, to which will be added a system to detect and foil guided missiles and tank rounds. There will also be a third layer, namely a hard kill system capable of destroying incoming munitions.

Finally, it is worth noting that while the Leclerc has an impressive specification, it has yet to be tried in combat. As such, it has not achieved the "Top Gun" status of other MBTs such as the Abrams, Challenger 2 and Merkava. The vehicle has been purchased by the United Arab Emirates.

RIGHT: **This impressive gathering of tanks and men is probably part of a French armoured regiment while on training. Each French Army regiment equipped with the Leclerc MBT has a total of 40 tanks – one at RHQ and three squadrons of 13 each.** BELOW: **A Leclerc ARV pulls a Leclerc MBT during a training exercise in Qatar. The first of these ARVs was completed in Spring 1994. As well as recovering disabled tanks and towing them to safety, the ARV has the necessary equipment to carry out repairs in forward areas, such as power pack changes.**

Leclerc MBT

Entered service: 1992
Crew: 3
Weight: 56,000kg/55.1 tons
Dimensions: Length – 9.87m/32ft 4.5in
    Height (over turret hatch) – 2.53m/8ft 3.5in
    Width – 3.71m/12ft 2in
Armament: Main – 120mm/4.72in gun
    Secondary – 1 x 12.7mm/0.5in and
    1 x 7.62mm/0.3in machine-guns
Armour: Unspecified
Powerplant: SACM V8X-1500 12-cylinder diesel,
    1,118.6kW/1,500hp
Performance: Speed – 72kph/44.7mph
    Range – 450km/279.6 miles

Leopard 1 Main Battle Tank

Originating from an earlier development project shared by Germany, France and Italy, the Leopard 1 was the German vehicle that resulted when that programme failed. First manufactured in 1963 by Krauss-Maffei of Munich, the initial design was influenced by the French AMX-30, where the armour was kept relatively light when compared with other contemporary MBTs in order to gain on mobility (although it was increased in later Marks).

With a weight of almost 40 tons and powered by a MTU MB 10-cylinder 618.9kW/830hp multi-fuel engine, it has a top speed of 65kph/40.4mph and a range of 600km/373 miles. The main armament is the British-made 105mm/4.13in rifled gun fitted with a gyroscopic stabilizer for accurate firing on the move. There are also two 7.62mm/0.3in machine-guns, one mounted coaxially. The vehicle has a crew of four and is fitted with automatic fire control, NBC (Nuclear, Biological and Chemical) protection and night-vision equipment.

With its good design and all-round reliability, the Leopard 1 has had a successful commercial history, over 6,000 vehicles being exported to nine NATO countries and also Australia, as well as being made under licence in Italy. Over its long lifespan the Leopard 1 has seen various extra armour upgrades and variants appear, including a mine-clearer and bulldozer. Though now replaced by Leopard 2 in the German Armed Forces, it is still in service with many other armies.

ABOVE: **This Leopard 1 is on training in the south of Holland.** BELOW: **Following rehabilitation, post-war German main battle tank development was initially a tripartite programme between Germany, Italy and France. For the Germans this resulted in Leopard 1, with Krauss-Maffei as prime contractor. Although it was a satisfactory tank, Leopard 1 was really too light and it lacked armoured protection. Nevertheless, it stayed in service up to the Leopard 1 A5 model at the end of the century. It is still in service worldwide although some, in places like Brazil and Chile, originate from other NATO countries rather than Germany.**

LEFT: **Excellent view of an Italian Leopard 1. They were not ordered until 1970, 720 being ordered and delivered. In addition MaK delivered a further 120 gun tanks, 69 ARVs and 12 AEVs.** ABOVE: **Leopard 1 could be fitted with a snorkel mast for deep wading.** BELOW: **As with Challenger, Leopard 1 had a driver training model where the turret was replaced by an observation cabin. German models still had the 105mm/4.13in gun barrel (Dutch and Belgian models did not).** BOTTOM LEFT: **Good internal view of a Leopard 1 turret.**

The first NATO country to place an order for Leopard 1 was Belgium (in 1967), and in all they have 334 gun tanks, plus a further 100 or more variants, of which 55 are the Gepard AA vehicle with twin 35mm/1.38in Oerlikon cannon. Next came the Netherlands, who ordered 468 Leopard 1s between 1968–70. Now, as well as the countries mentioned already, Canada, Denmark, Greece, Norway and Turkey have all purchased Leopard 1s from Germany, while Brazil has 87 from Belgium, and Chile has 200 from the Netherlands.

Kraus-Maffei Wegmann, who have factories in Munich and Kassel, still offer a wide range of modification kits for the Leopard 1 MBT which include: extra armour for the turret and mantlet; armoured skirts (side plates); automatic transmission; integral thermal imaging; snow grousers (plus stowage brackets on the glacis plate); a dozer blade (already adopted by Australia); additional external stowage boxes; tracks with replaceable track pads; and a fire-suppression system.

Leopard 1 MBT

Entered service: 1963
Crew: 4
Weight: 40,400kg/39.76 tons
Dimensions: Length – 9.54m/31ft 3.5in
    Height (over turret hatch) – 2.76m/9ft 0.5in
    Width – 3.41m/11ft 2.5in
Armament: Main – 105mm/4.13in gun
    Secondary – 2 x 7.62mm/0.3in machine-guns
Armour: Maximum – 70mm/2.76in
Powerplant: MTU MB 828 M500 multi-fuel,
    618.9kW/830hp
Performance: Speed – 65kph/40.4mph
    Range – 600km/373 miles

Leopard 2 Main Battle Tank

TOP AND ABOVE: **Excellent views of the Leopard 2 Main Battle Tank. It was in 1970 that Germany decided to proceed with a new MBT – the Leopard 2. Numerous production lots have since been built and taken into service with the German, Greek, Spanish, Dutch, Austrian, Danish, Finnish, Norwegian, Polish, Swiss and Swedish armies. In total, well over 1,000 have been produced, all built by Krauss-Maffei Wegmann GmbH. Leopard 2 is one of the finest MBTs currently in world service, and in addition to the gun tank, there are AVLBs, ARVs and driver training vehicles, while the latest developments involve the fitting of a new gun.**

The Leopard 2 is produced by Krauss-Maffei of Munich – and like the Leopard 1, originated in another failed, shared AFV project, this time between Germany and the USA, and known as the MBT 70. Using many components designed for that project, Leopard 2 emerged in 1979, after a spate of prototypes and intensive trials. The all-round quality of the Leopard 2's performance is indicative of the meticulous development cycle this vehicle has undergone. With upgrade packages including improved spaced armour, main gun, stabilization, suspension, navigation and fire control, it is still very much a contemporary "Top Gun" MBT.

Leopard 2 weighs almost 59 tons and is powered by an MTU MB 873 12-cylinder diesel engine, giving it a top speed of 72kph/44.7mph and a range of 550km/310.7 miles. The main armament was initially the L4, a Rheinmetall 120mm/4.72in smoothbore gun, but this has more recently been upgraded to the longer-barrelled L55. There are also two 7.62mm/0.3in machine-guns, one mounted coaxially to the main armament.

Used and manufactured under licence by many NATO member countries, the Leopard 2 has spawned many indigenous variants, mounting different extra armour, weapons and fire-control systems, or otherwise modified for a specific purpose such as the ARV (Armoured Recovery Vehicle) and mine-clearer versions. The Swiss Army now has about 400 Leopard 2 (Pz 87 Leo) MBTs, 60–70 per cent of which were built in Switzerland.

The latest model is the Leopard 2A5/2A6 MBT, which is virtually identical to its predecessor but has the following improvements: commander's roof-mounted periscope now has a thermal sight whose image is transmitted to a monitor inside the turret; all-new electrical gun control equipment has replaced the earlier hydraulic system, now quieter, easier to maintain and uses less electrical energy; improved armour protection for the frontal arc of the turret, giving it a distinctive arrowhead shape; new driver's hatch that slides to the right; TV camera installed at the rear of the hull to allow for safer reversing (it has a 65-degree field of view both in horizontal and vertical planes); a hybrid navigation system enabling the commander to navigate in any operational environment; and modifications to the laser range data processor.

There have also been a number of improvements to the Swedish Leopard 2 (known as Strv 122), which include: more protection to the front and sides of the chassis similar to that for the turret; improved roof protection against bomblets; and an eye-safe laser range finder.

TOP: **This Leopard 2 Main Battle Tank is one of about 400 ordered by the Swiss Army, the first being operational by early 1988.** ABOVE: **Leopard 2 deep-wading at the factory.** BELOW: **The Leopard 2 moving cross-country.**

Leopard 2 MBT

Entered service: 1979
Crew: 4
Weight: 59,700kg/58.76tons
Dimensions: Length – 9.97m/32ft 8.5in
　　　Height (over turret hatch) – 2.64m/8ft 8in
　　　Width – 3.74m/12ft 3in
Armament: Main – 120mm/4.72in gun
　　　Secondary – 2 x 7.62mm/0.3in machine-guns
Armour: Unspecified
Powerplant: MTU MB 873 Ka501 12-cylinder diesel,
　　　1,118.5kW/1,500hp
Performance: Speed – 72kph/44.7mph
　　　Range – 500km/310.7 miles

M41 Walker Bulldog Light Tank

Designed after the end of World War II to replace the M24 Chaffee, the M41 Walker Bulldog eventually surfaced in 1951 after an extensive period of prototype testing. With a weight of 23,495kg/23.1 tons, it was powered by a Continental AOS 95-3 6-cylinder supercharged petrol engine, delivering a top speed of 72.4kph/45mph, and had a range of 161km/ 100 miles. The main armament was a 76mm/2.99in main gun supplemented by two machine-guns, one of 12.7mm/ 0.5in and the other 7.62mm/0.3in.

The Walker Bulldog was fast and packed a powerful punch for its size. It saw action in Vietnam and served in many NATO member armies, as well as being exported to various countries in South America and Asia.

Some of these countries have carried out extensive modifications, as well as building "lookalikes" such as the Bernardini M41 manufactured in Brazil, while other extensive work was done in the 1980s by Spain to convert the M41 to an anti-tank role,

The Belgian company Cockerill successfully replaced the existing 76mm/2.99in main gun with a 90mm/3.54in, and that particular model was adopted by Uruguay.

Production of the Bulldog has long ceased, but the M41 is still to be found in service all over the world. Perhaps the strangest use for it was as a remote-controlled tank for testing air-to-ground missiles by the US Navy in the 1980s. It was also widely used for trial purposes by the USA, especially for work on the M551 Sheridan project. Modifications included a variety of weapons systems, including an Anti-Aircraft (AA) variant armed with twin 40mm/1.58in M2A1 Bofors AA guns.

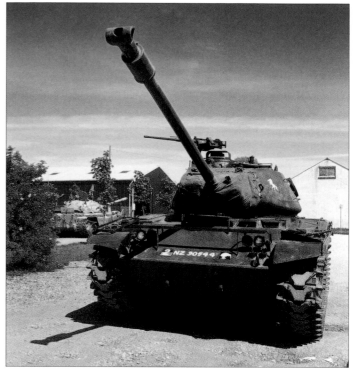

ABOVE: **American-built and widely sold overseas, more than 5,500 of these excellent little light tanks were built and exported, many fighting both in Korea and Vietnam, being one of the most effective weapons of the South Vietnamese. It mounted a 76mm/2.99in gun which had a good anti-armour performance. This M41 belonged to the New Zealand Armoured Corps.** BELOW: **The 23,495kg/ 23.1 ton M41 was a relatively easy transporter load, as is seen here. First production models appeared in 1951, there being three Marks (A1, A2 and A3), as well as the chassis being used for both AA and SP gun conversions.**

ABOVE: **The M41 was exported worldwide. In Brazil it was upgraded to the Bernardini M41 and serves both with the Brazil and Uruguay armies, mounting a 90mm/3.54in Cockerill gun.** RIGHT: **A breech-end view inside the turret of an M41 Walker Bulldog.** BELOW: **Realistic training in the USA included anti-gas exercises with both the infantry and tank crews wearing respirators.**

Fifty years after it was rushed into service, the Walker Bulldog still remains "on the books" of eight countries, five of which are in South America. Largest holdings, however, are currently in Taiwan – estimated to be between 400 and 675. With a new engine, performance of the tank has been greatly increased; for example, a maximum road speed of 72kph/45mph and a range of 450km/280 miles. The Walker Bulldog lives on!

M41 Walker Bulldog Light Tank

Entered service: 1951
Crew: 4
Weight: 23,495kg/23.1 tons
Dimensions: Length – 8.21m/26ft 11in
　　　　Height (over turret hatch) – 2.72m/8ft 11in
　　　　Width – 3.2m/10ft 6in
Armament: Main – 76mm/2.99in gun
　　　　Secondary – 1 x 12.7mm/0.5in and
　　　　1 x 7.62mm/0.3in machine-guns
Armour: Maximum – 32mm/1.26in
Powerplant: Continental AOS 95-3 petrol,
　　　　372.9kW/500hp
Performance: Speed – 72.4kph/45mph
　　　　Range – 161km/100 miles

M47 Medium (Patton) Tank

Named after the famous US World War II General, George S. Patton, the M47 was the first truly post-war American tank to be produced, being rushed into production during the Korean crisis in 1952. Its interim predecessor, the M46, which was to all intents and purposes an improved M26 Pershing, did fight in Korea and was also known as the Patton.

The M47 was based on the M46 hull with a newly designed turret, and weighed 46,165kg/45.4 tons. Using a torsion bar suspension system and powered by a Continental AVDS

1790 5B 12-cylinder supercharged petrol engine, it had a top speed of 48kph/29.8mph and a range of 129km/80.1 miles. The new cast turret made the M47 easily identifiable, as it bulged out to the rear and tapered sharply to the front to a small mantlet mounting the M36 90mm/3.54in main gun. For the secondary armament there were two Browning machine-guns, one of 12.7mm/0.5in and the other 7.62mm/0.3in.

The M47 was the last American tank with a five-man crew and it did not have NBC (Nuclear, Biological and Chemical) protection, night-fighting or computerized fire-control systems, so it could not fire accurately while on the move. It proved to be a stopgap development soon invalidated by the advent of the M48.

Although it did not serve for long with US forces, it was exported extensively to her allies, including Taiwan, Greece, Iran, Italy, Japan, Jordan, Netherlands, Pakistan, Portugal, Saudi Arabia, South Korea, Spain, Turkey and Yugoslavia. A final upgrade programme began in the late 1960s, resulting in the M47M, using the engine and fire-control system from the M60A1 to further extend this vehicle's operational life.

There were some faults with the M47 that were recognized even before production began. Indeed, work had already

ABOVE AND LEFT: **First of the truly post-war American tanks was the 90mm/3.54in gun tank, designated as the M47, but popularly known as the Patton after the famous General George S. Patton, Jnr, who had been killed in a road accident in 1945. It would soon be replaced by the M48, also called the Patton.**

ABOVE: **Trials took place to fit the British 105mm/4.13in L7A1 tank gun into the M47s in service with the Italian Army, which proved to be very successful because the up-gunned result was much more stable. The M47s in Spanish service were fitted with the Rheinmetall 105mm/4.13in smoothbore gun (known as the M47-E2).** RIGHT: **This highly painted M46 is located at the Tank Museum, Bovington. The M47 used the same hull.** BELOW: **Part of a tank company of M47s on the firing line at the Armor School, Fort Knox, Kentucky, 1953.**

begun on its successor while it was being accepted by the US Army Equipment Review Board. For example, it was clear that turret protection was generally lower than that of the hull and that the fuel carried was insufficient to last through a normal battlefield day. It would never see action with the regular US Army and would soon be relegated to the National Guard (November 1953). In fact, it was a better training vehicle because its five-man crew (the M48 had only four) meant that 20 per cent more men could be trained in each training cycle.

M47 Medium (Patton) Tank

Entered service: 1952
Crew: 5
Weight: 46,165kg/45.4 tons
Dimensions: Length – 8.56m/28ft 1in
Height (over turret hatch) – 3.35m/11ft
Width – 3.2m/10ft 6in
Armament: Main – 90mm/3.54in M36 gun
Secondary – 1 x 12.7mm/0.5in and 1 x 7.62mm/0.3in machine-guns
Armour: Maximum – 115mm/4.53in
Powerplant: Continental AVDS 1790 5B V12 petrol, 604kW/810hp
Performance: Speed – 48kph/29.8mph
Range – 129km/80.1 miles

M48 Patton Main Battle Tank

The M48 Patton Main Battle Tank was another American tank to be rushed into production during the Korean crisis, and it initially suffered from teething problems as a consequence. However, it went on to have a long and distinguished service life, including combat with US forces in Vietnam.

It had a lower wider hull than the previous M47, along with a new, less bulging turret, with a visually distinctive and powerful searchlight just above the main gun. Weighing 48,987kg/48.2 tons, the M48 was powered by a Continental AVDS 1790 2 12-cylinder engine, giving it a top speed of 48kph/29.8mph and a range of 499km/310.1 miles.

The main armament of the M48 was a 90mm/3.54in gun, supplemented by a 7.62mm/0.3in coaxial machine-gun and a 12.7mm/0.5in anti-aircraft machine-gun mounted on the commander's cupola.

It was one of the first tanks to have an analogue mechanical fire-control system and saw various upgrades. These included different engines, suspension, fire-control and weapons systems, and main armament, which was upgraded to a 105mm/4.13in gun almost immediately. The M48 was very popular on the US export market, being supplied to many countries worldwide. Some of these customers modified it extensively for their own use, including Spain, Israel and Taiwan.

ABOVE AND BELOW: **The M48 Patton tank was originally armed with a 90mm/3.54in gun, later to be replaced by a 105mm/4.13in gun. Despite being rushed into service in 1952 and having some faults, the Patton was a popular tank, with large numbers being built (over 11,000). It was produced in five Marks (up to A5) and sold to Greece, Germany, South Korea, Spain, Taiwan, Turkey, Iran and Israel.**

Starting in 1958, the West German army was supplied with a total of 1,400 M48 series AFVs, including armoured recovery vehicles (M88), M55 SP howitzers and M48 AVLB as well as gun tanks. It is also most interesting to note that subsequently, after fruitless negotiations direct with the USA, Israel was able to obtain their first M48s from the Germans, a party of selected Israeli tank officers being trained on a crash course in great secrecy in Germany!

The Taiwanese M48H, also known as Brave Tiger, was produced in 1990 by combining M60 hulls with M48 turrets, mounting an indigenously built version of the 105mm/4.13in rifled main gun, along with other elements including digital fire control and sight stabilization from the Abrams M1.

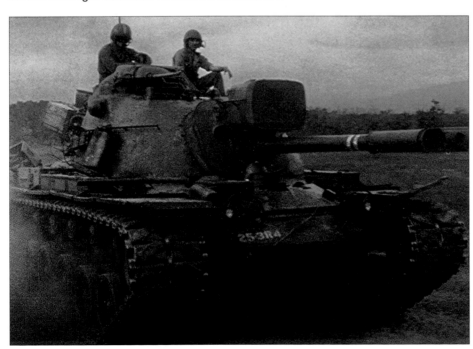

TOP LEFT: **The Tank Museum's M48 in a display of NATO tanks.** ABOVE LEFT: **The M67 flamethrower version of the M48 is seen here in Vietnam in 1968 in the act of using its flamethrower. None of this model are still in service.** ABOVE: **The M48H, also known as Brave Tiger, was a modified M48 with a home-produced version of the British 105mm/4.13in gun. The tank actually uses the hulls of the US M60, M60A1, M60A3, as well as the M48A5 and South Korean K1. In addition, it is said that some Merkava Marks 1 and 2 are also employed, so it really is a hybrid!** LEFT: **An M48 moving into action in Vietnam. M48A1, A2 and A3 all saw active service there, as did the M48 AVLB and M88 recovery vehicle.**

M48 Patton MBT

Entered service: 1953
Crew: 4
Weight: 48,987kg/48.2 tons
Dimensions: Length – 9.31m/30ft 6.5in
    Height (over turret hatch) – 3.01m/9ft 10.5in
    Width – 3.63m/11ft 11in
Armament: Main – 105mm/4.13in L7 gun
    Secondary – 1 x 12.7mm/0.5in and 1 x
    7.62mm/0.3in machine-guns
Armour: Maximum – 180mm/7.07in
Powerplant: Continental AVDS 1790 2 12-cylinder
    diesel, 559.3kW/750hp
Performance: Speed – 48kph/29.8mph
    Range – 499km/310.1 miles

M50 Ontos Tank Destroyer

In the mid-1950s the USA developed the M50 Ontos (*Ontos* is Greek for "thing") as an early attempt to provide rapidly deployable air-portable firepower for airborne troops. It was based on the chassis of the T55/T56 series of experimental vehicles, combined with a new a distinctive pyramidal mini-turret which mounted six 106mm/4.17in M40A1 recoilless (RCR) rifles, three to a side, firing mainly HEAT (High-Explosive Anti-Tank) but also anti-personnel munitions. These weapons were aimed by using a Spotting Rifle fitted to the top tubes which was fired first to determine the range and bearing of the target, the six recoilless rifles then being discharged singly or en masse.

The Ontos weighed 8,641kg/8.5 tons, had a crew of three and was powered by a Chrysler V8 engine, giving it a speed of 48kph/30mph and a range of 241km/ 150 miles. This vehicle suffered from a number of serious disadvantages: the loader was vulnerable to enemy fire when reloading the weapons system because he had to get out of the vehicle; the recoilless rifles lacked any real accuracy; and there was a massive and dangerous back-blast from the rifle tubes when discharged.

The Ontos was really only a stopgap measure, with as few as 300 being made before it was discontinued. It saw action only briefly in Vietnam, where it was used by troops on the ground primarily in an artillery mode from prepared firebases. In 1966 the engine was upgraded to the Chrysler V8, generating 134.2kW/180hp, but the vehicle was soon superseded and withdrawn from service in 1970 to be replaced by other air-portable alternatives offering more firepower and protection.

ABOVE AND BELOW LEFT: **Designed in the mid-1950s as a small air-portable tank destroyer, Ontos (Greek for "thing") comprised six 106mm/4.17in recoilless rifles mounted on a modified APC chassis. While the US Army dropped the idea in preference for Jeep-mounted recoilless rifles, the USMC avidly seized on the proposal, and it went into production in 1955, some 300 being built. It saw action in Dominica and Vietnam and knocked out various light tanks (e.g. AMX-13). It was retired in the late 1960s. It was also used for experiments with titanium armour as the T55 Ontos APC, while another version proposed was a light assault vehicle, armed with four or eight machine-guns. Finally, there were three more proposals, all with various anti-tank guns. None were ever built.**

M50 Ontos TD 🇺🇸

Entered service: 1955
Crew: 3
Weight: 8,641kg/8.5 tons
Dimensions: Length – 3.83m/12ft 7in
　　Height (over turret hatch) – 2.13m/7ft
　　Width – 2.60m/8ft 6.5in
Armament: Main – 6 x 106mm/4.17in recoilless rifles
　　Secondary – 7.62mm/0.3in machine-gun
Armour: Maximum – 13mm/0.51in
Powerplant: General Motors 302 V6 petrol, 108.1kW/145hp
Performance: Speed – 48kph/29.8mph
　　Range – 241km/149.8 miles

LEFT AND BELOW LEFT:

Another light airborne support weapon was the Scorpion 90mm/ 3.54in anti-tank gun mounted on an all aluminium hull and weighing a total of just 7,144kg/7 tons. Its major drawbacks were the lack of crew protection and a vulnerable petrol engine. It was soon replaced by the M551 Sheridan.

M56 Scorpion Tank Destroyer

Known officially as the M56 Self-Propelled Anti-Tank (SPAT), the M56 was another US attempt at developing air-portable firepower during the 1950s for use with rapidly deployable troops.

To save on weight, the vehicle had an aluminium hull and no turret, with only a small gun-shield for protection – an approach that didn't endear it to the troops that had to operate it. It was actually based on the unarmoured chassis of the M76 amphibious cargo carrier, the gun being on a low pedestal mount on top of the hull, which carried four road-wheels on either side suspended by torsion bars.

The engine, driver and his controls took up all of the remaining space in the hull, leaving the gun-layer to ride on top of the vehicle. Where the remaining two crewmen travelled is not clear, although logically they must have gone with any ammunition vehicle attached to the detachment. Presumably when the Scorpion went into action and they had to change position, they would simply hang on to the outside as best they could! At 7,144kg/7 tons, the M56 was powered by a Continental AOI-4025 6-cylinder petrol engine, giving it a top speed of 45kph/28mph and a range of 225km/139.8 miles. It mounted a 90mm/3.54in M54 main gun and saw action in Vietnam, where it tended to be used as a support weapon in a prepared position.

Under-armoured, under-powered and unpopular, it was soon replaced by the M551 Sheridan.

M56 Scorpion TD	

Entered service: 1953
Crew: 4
Weight: 7,144kg/7 tons
Dimensions: Length – 5.84m/19ft 2in
Height (over turret hatch) – 2.05m/6ft 8.5in
Width – 2.57m/8ft 5in
Armament: Main – 90mm/3.54in M54 gun
Armour: None
Powerplant: Continental AOI-4025 6-cylinder petrol, 149.kW/200hp
Performance: Speed – 45kph/28mph
Range – 225km/139.8 miles

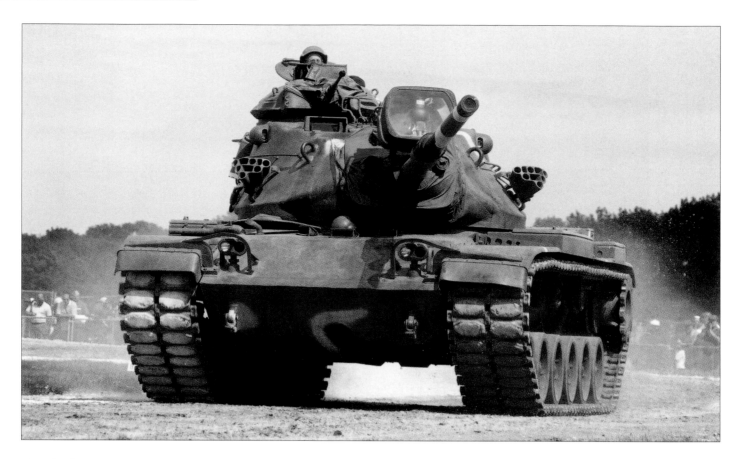

M60 Main Battle Tank

Manufactured by General Dynamics, the M60 is one of the world's most successful MBTs, with over 15,000 built. First entering service with the US Army in 1960, it went on to serve in the armies of at least 22 countries. The tank has provided excellent battlefield performance over four decades and has been continuously advanced and upgraded with appliqué armour, increasingly powerful engines, new guns and fire-control systems, ammunition and other features.

Weighing almost 52 tons and with a crew of four, the M60 is powered by a Continental AVDS 1790 2A V12 turbo-charged diesel engine, giving it a top speed of 48kph/29.8mph and a range of 500km/310.7 miles. The main armament is the 105mm/4.13in M68 rifled gun derived from the L7A1 105mm/4.13in gun of the British Centurion, along with two machine-guns – a coaxial 7.62mm/0.3in M240 and a 12.7mm/0.5in.

The M60A1, with a new turret and thicker armour, was manufactured from 1962 to 1980. The M60A2, with a new turret mounting a 152mm/5.98in gun and missile launcher, was produced in 1972. From 1978 to 1987 the M60A3, with improvements to its fire control, was the most successful and numerously produced of the series.

ABOVE AND LEFT: **Two views of the Tank Museum's M60 Main Battle Tank, including one of it going through a "wall of fire". The M60 was approved in the late 1950s and the contract awarded to Chrysler in 1959. Since then, over 5,400 have been built for the US forces and many thousands sold worldwide, the Israelis being the next largest user. The tank has a 105mm/4.13in gun and a very prominent searchlight.**

ABOVE: **An IDF (Israeli Defence Force) M60 moves into battle with some extra passengers.** LEFT: **Hard at work building M60 turrets in the Chrysler factory.** BELOW: **The M60A1 fitted with ERA (Explosive Reactive Armour). A small number of USMC M60A1s were used during Operation "Desert Storm" in 1991. The Israeli-invented ERA gives added protection to vulnerable areas such as the turret.**

Having such a long front-line life in so many countries, the M60 has seen many variants, modifications and enhancements, with Israel in particular upgrading M60s into their own types, including the Magach and the Sabra. With so many countries still fielding M60s, General Dynamics Land Systems (GDLS) has recently brought out the M60-2000 upgrade package, using the turret and 120mm/4.72in M256 smoothbore main gun of the M1 Abrams, along with a new up-rated engine, fire-control and safety systems. In this way the service life of this excellent MBT has been prolonged still further.

M60A1 MBT

Entered service: 1960
Crew: 4
Weight: 52,617kg/51.8 tons
Dimensions: Length – 9.44m/31ft
  Height (over turret hatch) – 3.27m/10ft 8.5in
  Width – 3.63m/11ft 11in
Armament: Main – 105mm/4.13in M68 gun
  Secondary – 1 x 12.7mm/0.5in and
  1 x 7.62mm/0.3in machine-guns
Armour: Maximum – 143mm/5.63in
Powerplant: Continental AVDS 1790 2A V12 diesel,
  559.3kW/750hp
Performance: Speed – 48kph/29.8mph
  Range – 500km/310.7 miles

LEFT: **A US Army M60 takes cover in a corn field during a NATO exercise in the 1960–70s, being totally ignored by the farmer and his wife!**

LEFT: **The Sheridan Light Tank. Worried by the ever increasing size and weight of modern main battle tanks, the Sheridan was a US attempt to combine a gun and missile system in one 152mm/5.98in launcher. The 15,830kg/15.6-ton light tank had a crew of four and was developed in 1959.**

BELOW: **Good photograph of an anti-armour Shillelagh missile being launched. The Sheridan continued to serve until the 1990s.**

M551 Sheridan Light Tank

The M551 Sheridan is yet another air-portable American light tank developed for its airborne divisions to replace the unsatisfactory M56 Scorpion. Entering service in 1968 with a weight of 15,830kg/15.6 tons and a crew of four, the Sheridan was powered by a Detroit Diesel 6V-53T 6-cylinder turbocharged engine, giving it a top speed of 72kph/44.7mph and a range of 600km/372.9 miles.

The main armament was the MGM-51 Shillelagh tube-launched, wire-guided missile system, which could also fire 152mm/5.98in shells, along with a

7.62mm/0.3in machine-gun for close-quarter protection. However, there were lots of problems with this weapons system, which held up the vehicle's entry into service and plagued it thereafter.

It was also lightly armoured with aluminium to save on weight, and as a consequence very vulnerable to a whole range of weapons. During combat in Vietnam the missile system was soon rejected in favour of more conventional munitions, but the Sheridan still did not perform well, being adversely affected by the moist conditions and, with little

protection on its hull bottom, it was very vulnerable to mines. Nevertheless, the Sheridan continued in service until the 1990s; for example, 82 Airborne Division's Sheridans were among the first AFVs to arrive in the Persian Gulf in 1990.

M551 Sheridan Light Tank	

Entered service: 1968
Crew: 4
Weight: 15,830kg/15.6 tons
Dimensions: Length – 6.30m/20ft 8in
 Height (over turret hatch) – 2.95m/9ft 8in
 Width – 2.82m/9ft 3in
Armament: Main – 152mm/5.98in gun/ missile system
 Secondary – 7.62mm/0.3in machine-gun
Armour: Unspecified
Powerplant: Detroit Diesel 6V-53T 6-cylinder diesel, 223.7kW/300hp
Performance: Speed – 72kph/44.7mph
 Range – 600km/372.9 miles

LEFT: **The missile system was the 152mm/5.98in Shillelagh missile system, whose HEAT warhead could knock out any known tank. Sheridan was swiftly deployed in Vietnam. The missile guidance system was withdrawn and replaced by the "beehive" anti-personnel round, but this also led to many problems.**

LEFT: **The Israeli name for their upgrade of the American M60 MBT was Magach, a Hebrew acronym for the Jewish letters: Mem and Chaf plus the middle letter "Gimel" which stands for "Germany", the first source of Israeli M48s. Latest of the continuing upgrades is Magach 7, which is fitted with passive armour to its hull and turret.** BELOW LEFT: **Another view of the M60 Magach. This was the first version specifically up-armoured for urban combat.**

Magach Main Battle Tank

The Magach is the Israeli Defence Force (IDF) name for what was the Patton M48/M60 MBT series of US tanks which have been in active service with the Israeli armoured forces for over 30 years. In that time they have undergone sustained indigenous modification and enhancement to keep the Magach as a state-of-the-art weapons system, continuously tried and tested in combat.

Armed with the original 90mm/3.54in main gun, they first saw action during the 1967 Six Day War and were then upgraded (Magach 3 and 5) with a new 105mm/4.13in M68 L7 gun (as carried by the Centurion) and used in the 1968 War of Attrition. Deployed in time for the 1973 Yom Kippur War, the M60 (Magach 6 and 7) models went on to become the mainstay of the IDF's armoured corps

for many years. These Magachs were upgraded with Explosive Reactive Armour (ERA), new engines, tracks and improved fire control and then used in the 1982 Israeli Invasion of Lebanon.

The Magach 7 had further new upgrade suites, some of which could be retrofitted to earlier versions, including engine and transmission packs, passive armour, optical systems, ranging and new fire-control systems, NBC (Nuclear, Biological and Chemical) protection, fire suppression, navigation and weapons systems.

Magach MBT

Entered service: 1970

Crew: 4

Weight: 54,857kg/54 tons

Dimensions: Length – 8.56m/28ft 1in
Height (over turret hatch) – 3.35m/11ft
Width – 3.2m/10ft 6in

Armament: Main – 90mm/3.54in and then 105mm/4.13in gun
Secondary – 3 x 7.62mm/0.3in machine-guns, 1 x 12.7mm/0.5in coaxial machine-gun above main gun

Armour: Maximum – 115mm/4.53in

Powerplant: General Dynamics AVDS 1790 A V12 diesel, 677.1kW/908hp

Performance: Speed – 48kph/29.8mph
Range – 129km/80.6 miles

Merkava Main Battle Tank

The Merkava (Chariot) is an unusual MBT of innovative design, attributed to the Major General Israel Tal of the IDF's (Israeli Defence Force) Armoured Corps, which places special emphasis on crew protection. To further this aim, the engine is located in the front of the vehicle and special attention has been paid to the siting of extra-spaced armour on the frontal arc, the side skirts and track protectors, and the bulkheads between the crew and the fuel and ammunition. There is even a special protective umbrella for the tank

commander when his hatch is open. Another unusual feature is that the tank has rear doors in the hull, enabling it either to carry extra ammunition or a small squad of infantry.

The Merkava Mark 1 came into service in 1979, when 40 tanks were delivered to 7th Armoured Brigade. Weighing 60,963kg/60 tons and powered by a TCM diesel AVDS 1790 9AR engine delivering a top speed of 46kph/28.6mph and a range of 400km/248.5 miles, the Mark 1 mounted a 105mm/4.13in main gun along with a coaxial 7.62mm/0.3in machine-gun and a 12.7mm/0.5in commander's machine-gun. The Merkava Mark 2 had increased engine performance, which gave it a top speed of 55kph/34mph and a range 500km/310 miles. Merkava first saw action in Lebanon, between April and June 1982.

ABOVE: **No nation has more post-war armoured battle experience than the Israelis, who have been fighting almost non-stop since 1948. It was in 1967 after the Six Day War that they decided to design and build their own main battle tank, the revolutionary Merkava, test rigs being based on both the M48 and Centurion, under the expert eye of General Israel Tal. First production models appeared in 1978, but the MBT did not see action until 1982 in Lebanon. This photograph is of a Merkava Mark 2.** LEFT: **An impressive line-up of Merkava Mark 2s, which weighed over 60 tons and mounted a 105mm/4.13in rifled gun.**

ABOVE: **This Merkava Mark 2 was photographed in Lebanon during Operation "Peace for Galilee".** RIGHT: **An early Mark 1 on show at the IDF Tank Museum at Latrun.** BELOW: **A Mark 3, known as Baz (Hawk), which mounts a 120mm/4.72in smoothbore gun, a modular armour suite and an improved suspension.**

New suites covering the various elements of the tank are constantly being updated in the light of combat experience. For Merkava Mark 3 these included a new suspension system, a 894.8kW/1,200hp engine and new transmission, an upgraded 120mm/4.72in main gun developed by Israel Military Industries with a thermal sleeve to increase accuracy by preventing heat distortion, and ballistic protection provided by further special add-on armour modules. The Merkava Mark 4 has further improved night and remote vision devices, a new MTU 1,118.5kW/1,500hp diesel engine, an enhanced main gun package and increased modular passive armour.

Merkava Mark 3 MBT	✡

Entered service: 1977 (Mark 1)
Crew: 4
Weight: 62,000kg/61.02 tons
Dimensions: Length – 7.6m/24ft 11in
    Height (over turret hatch) – 2.64m/8ft 8in
    Width – 3.7m/12ft 1.5in
Armament: Main – 120mm/4.72in gun
    Secondary – 3 x 7.62mm/0.3in machine-guns
Armour: Unspecified
Powerplant: Teledyne AVDS 1790 9AR V12 diesel, 894.8kW/1,200hp
Performance: Speed – 55kph/34.2mph
    Range – 500km/310.7 miles

Main Battle Tank 70

The MBT-70 was a joint US–German heavy tank project that was launched in the 1960s and formed the source vehicle for both the Abrams M1 and Leopard 2 main battle tanks. The MBT-70 incorporated some radical new design elements, including a main

gun that could fire wire-guided missile munitions as well as conventional rounds, and a bustle-mounted automatic loading system for the main gun, thereby doing away with the need for a loader and reducing the crew to three.

Weighing 46,000kg/45.3 tons, equipped with hydro-pneumatic suspension and powered by a Continental AVCR 12-cylinder multi-fuel engine, the MBT-70 had a top speed of 70kph/43.5mph and a range of 650km/403.9 miles. The American model mounted the 152mm/5.98in gun/missile system – as later fitted to the Sheridan M551 – while the German version had a 120mm/4.72in smoothbore main armament – both with

ABOVE: **In 1963, West Germany and the USA signed an agreement to build a main battle tank which they called MBT-70. While it had many innovative modern features, agreement on a standardized vehicle could not be reached, and the project was eventually cancelled in 1970. Nevertheless, numerous features were brought forward into the two nations' tank-building programmes for the Abrams and the Leopard 2.**

LEFT AND BELOW LEFT: **Two photographs of MBT-70 pilot number two which shows the tank with the fire-control equipment installed.**

a state-of-the-art digital fire-control and gun-stabilization system. However, in the end the two countries could not agree on a standardized vehicle, so in 1970 the project was cancelled and each partner went their own way to develop individual main battle tanks.

MBT-70

Entered service: 1967 (prototypes only)
Crew: 3
Weight: 46,000kg/45.3 tons
Dimensions: Length – 6.99m/22ft 11in
  Height (over turret hatch) – 2.59m/8ft 6in
  Width – 3.51m/11ft 6in
Armament: Main – 152mm/5.98in gun/missile system or 120mm/4.72in smoothbore gun
  Secondary – 7.62mm/0.3in machine-gun
Armour: Unspecified
Powerplant: Continental AVCR 12-cylinder multi-fuel, 1,099.9kW/1,475hp
Performance: Speed – 70kph/43.5mph
  Range – 650km/403.9 miles

Olifant Medium Tank

The South African Olifant is a Centurion-derived medium tank which became the mainstay of the South African armoured forces for a long period of time. The Olifant was made in South Africa by Vickers OMC Company in conjunction with the larger British parent Vickers. Since its introduction in the 1980s it has undergone various upgrades and enhancements to maintain it as a viable battlefield weapons system.

Weighing over 55 tons and powered by a V12 diesel engine with a top speed of 45kph/28mph and a range of 500km/310.6 miles, the Olifant has a crew of four and mounts as its main armament either the LIW GT-7 105mm/4.13in, or a LIW proprietary 120mm/4.72in smoothbore tank gun. Either of these is fitted into a newly designed turret incorporating a bustle-mounted ammunition carousel and all the latest fire-control and safety features, including blow-off panels on the turret deck.

The latest model (Mark 1B) also boasts a new power pack, new torsion bar suspension, new electronic systems and modular add-on-armour packages.

In addition to the gun tank, there are ARV (Armoured Recovery Vehicle), AVLB (Armoured Vehicle Launched Bridge) and mine-clearing variants.

ABOVE AND RIGHT: **Designed in 1976 and based on the British Centurion, the South African Olifant (Elephant), weighs 56,000kg/55.1 tons, has a crew of four and mounts a 105mm/4.13in gun. The latest version (the Mark 1B) has numerous modern features. South Africa has a total of 224 Olifant Mark 1A and 1Bs in service.**

LEFT: **In addition to the gun tank, there are ARVs, AVLBs and mine-clearing vehicles. The ARV seen here is based upon an Olifant Mark 1A.**

Olifant Medium Tank

Entered service: 1980
Crew: 4
Weight: 56,000kg/55.1 tons
Dimensions: Length – 8.29m/27ft 2.5in
  Height (over turret hatch) – 2.94m/9ft 7.5in
  Width – 3.39m/11ft 1.5in
Armament: Main – 105mm/4.13in LIW GT-7
  or 120mm/4.72in LIW gun
  Secondary – 2 x 7.62mm/0.3in machine-guns
Armour: Unspecified
Powerplant: V12 diesel, delivering 708.4kW/950hp
Performance: Speed – 45kph/28mph
  Range – 500km/310.6 miles

LEFT: **It was the German company Rheinmetall who developed the TAM (*Tanque Argentino Mediano*) to meet the requirements of the Argentine Army, the first prototype being produced in 1976. The TAM had a crew of four, an all-up weight of 30,000kg/ 29.53 tons and mounted a 105mm/4.13in rifled gun. The original requirement was for 512 TAM medium tanks and tracked armoured personnel carriers, but for financial reasons only about 350 were built. Some recent reports, however, indicate that production may well have recommenced.**

TAMSE TAM Medium Tank

The TAM was initially designed and produced by the German arms company Rheinmetall and then by TAMSE in Argentina to replace Argentina's ageing fleet of M4 Shermans. A critical factor in the selection of this tank by the Argentines was meeting the weight restrictions imposed by the country's bridge and road infrastructure. Following on from prototype testing in the mid-1970s, the vehicle was accepted and production began in Argentina under licence. The TAM was first delivered to the Argentine amoured forces in the early 1980s, although none saw action in the Falklands War in 1982.

Weighing almost 30 tons and with a crew of four, the TAM is powered by a MTU 6-cylinder diesel engine, giving it a top speed of 75kph/46.6mph and a range of 940km/584.1 miles. The chassis of the vehicle was based on the Marder APC, which was also

manufactured by Rheinmetall but with a newly designed three-man turret mounting a 105mm/4.13in rifled main gun and a 7.62mm/0.3in coaxial machine-gun, with another 7.62mm/0.3in gun mounted on the turret roof for anti-aircraft and close-quarter defence. The TAM also has modern gun stabilization,

fire-control, communications and safety equipment, and variants so far produced include a self-propelled howitzer, an ARV (Armoured Recovery Vehicle) and a multiple-launch rocket system. However, it is no longer being marketed and the manufacturer TAMSE has gone out of business.

LEFT: **Other versions included the Israeli LAR 160 multiple rocket system, the original turret being replaced by two 18-round launcher pods. It is thought that a small number of these were delivered to the Argentine Army.** BELOW LEFT: **The TAM on trials in Thailand in 1978 when the potential export model was known as the TH 301.**

TAMSE TAM Medium Tank	
Entered service: 1976	
Crew: 4	
Weight: 30,000kg/29.53 tons	
Dimensions: Length – 6.77m/22ft 3in	
Height (over turret hatch) – 2.71m/8ft 10.5in	
Width – 3.92m/10ft 10.5in	
Armament: Main – 105mm/4.13in gun	
Secondary – 2 x 7.62mm/0.3in machine-guns	
Armour: Unspecified	
Powerplant: MTU MB 833 Ka500 diesel, 536.9kW/720hp	
Performance: Speed – 75kph/46.6mph	
Range – 940km/584.1 miles	

LEFT, BELOW AND BOTTOM LEFT:
The Lenin Heavy Tank
was to all intents and
purposes the last in the
Soviet World War II heavy
tank series, being a
redesign of the JS-4 but
incorporating lessons
learned in the early post-
war years. In fact, it was
heavy, large and not as
easy to move around the
countryside as the more
modern medium tanks
such as the T-62,
which replaced it in
the mid-1960s.

T-10 Lenin Heavy Tank

Last in the KV and JS series of heavy tanks originating in the 1930s and being developed through World War II, the T-10 (also known as the Lenin) replaced the short-lived JS-4. Entering service in 1953, weighing 52,000kg/ 51.2 tons and fitted with torsion bar suspension, it was powered by the V12 diesel engine originally developed for the JS-4, providing a top speed of 42kph/26.1mph and a range of 250km/ 155.3 miles.

The T-10 was manned by a crew of four, protected by armour up to 270mm/ 10.63in thick on the frontal arc and armed with a D74 122mm/4.8in main gun

in a classic Soviet "mushroom head" turret which was sited well forward on the hull. There were also two 14.55mm/ 0.57in machine-guns and an optional extra 12.7mm/0.5in anti-aircraft machine-gun mounted outside on the commander's cupola.

The main drawback of the Lenin was its very limited ammunition stowage capacity of fewer than 30 rounds, although this was increased later to 50. The reality

was that the T-10 Lenin belonged to a previous generation of AFV made obsolete by new types of armour and ammunition that were enabling a new type of faster, lighter tank such as the T-62 to take on the role of the older classic heavies.

T-10 Lenin Heavy Tank

Entered service: 1953
Crew: 4
Weight: 52,000kg/51.2 tons
Dimensions: Length – 7.41m/24ft 3.5in
  Height (over turret hatch) – 2.43m/7ft 11.5in
  Width – 3.56m/11ft 8in
Armament: Main – 122mm/4.8in gun
  Secondary – 2 x 14.55mm/0.57in and
  1 x 12.7mm/0.3in machine-guns
Armour: Maximum – 270mm/10.63in
Powerplant: V2IS 12-cylinder diesel, 514.5kW/690hp
Performance: Speed – 42kph/26.1mph
  Range – 250km/155.3 miles

T–54/T–55 Medium Tank

This series of AFV ranks as one of the most prolific in terms of the sheer numbers produced, with some estimates as high as 60,000. It became the primary MBT of post-World War II Soviet tank forces and their satellite and client states all over the world for at least two decades. It was also built under licence in Czechoslovakia, Poland and China, and did not go out of production in the USSR until early in the 1990s.

The T-54 had a low-silhouette hull with a classic Soviet "mushroom dome" turret, weighed over 35 tons and was powered by a V54 V12 diesel engine, giving it a top speed of 48kph/29.8mph and a range 400km/248.5 miles. It was armed with a D10 100mm/3.94in rifled main gun, along with

ABOVE AND BELOW LEFT: **Following on from their highly successful wartime T-34/76 and T-34/85, the Soviets produced what must have been their most successful medium tanks ever – the T-54 and T-55 – with production starting in 1947. Estimates of the numbers produced since then must be in the region of 60,000, a staggering number, and even more than the wartime Sherman M4 Medium Tanks.**

a 7.62mm/0.3in coaxial machine-gun. Early versions also mounted a fixed 7.62mm/0.3in machine-gun in the bow, which was operated by the driver.

New models featured improvements as they came into service – beginning with night-vision equipment and an extra machine-gun for anti-aircraft defense, and going on to full-blown upgrade programmes with fire-control, navigation, communication and safety systems, as well as add-on armour suites. There were also the inevitably endless variants of an AFV whose use was so widespread and culturally diverse.

With the advent of the T-55 in the 1950s, the main flaw of the T54 – its automotive unreliability – was tackled with the fitting of a larger V255 V12 water-cooled diesel engine, thereby increasing the power, speed (50kph/31.1mph) and range (500km/310.7 miles) of the vehicle. There was also a new turret fitted – still a mushroom – without the loader's cupola or the prominent roof-top ventilator dome, and with two enlarged "D" roof panels. It also mounted an infrared gunner's searchlight above the main gun, but this was retrofitted to the T-54 and so is not a distinctive feature.

LEFT: **Many of these "rough and ready", highly reliable and easy-to-crew main battle tanks are still in service worldwide, with many having been sold off by European armies as they took on more sophisticated MBTs. The all-welded steel hull is divided into three compartments – driving at the front, fighting in the centre and engine at the rear.**
BELOW: **Russian tank crews working on their vehicles in their tank hangar.**

Again, improved models surfaced regularly, sporting an array of enhancements and variants, including further engine tweaks, NBC (Nuclear, Biological and Chemical) protection, add-on armour suites – especially ERA (Explosive Reactive Armour) – new main gun stabilization and fire-control systems.

Civilian conversions

Although the original production finished long ago, the T-54/T-55 is still in service with armies all over the world – a staggering 65 at last count – so it must be one of the most successful tanks ever built. Remarkably, the RFAS has also now started marketing a number of systems based on the T-54/T-55 MBT with purely civilian applications. These mainly centre around fire-fighting.

RIGHT AND BELOW: **The all-welded steel hull is divided into three compartments – driving at the front, fighting in the centre and engine at the rear. There are a wide variety of models of this 36,000kg/35.4-ton four-man tank, both T-54 and T-55 being armed with a 100mm/3.94in rifled gun.**

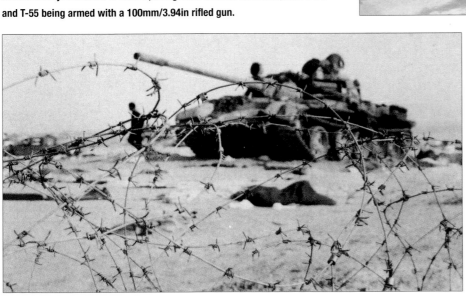

T-54/T-55 Medium Tank

Entered service: 1948
Crew: 4
Weight: 36,000kg/35.4 tons
Dimensions: Length – 6.45m/21ft 2in
Height (over turret hatch) – 2.4m/7ft 10.5in
Width – 3.27m/10ft 8.5in
Armament: Main – 100mm/3.94in gun
Secondary – 2 x 7.62mm/0.3in and
1 x 12.7mm/0.5in machine-guns
Armour: Maximum – 203mm/7.99in
Powerplant: V54 12-cylinder diesel, generating
387.8kW/520hp
Performance: Speed – 48kph/29.8mph
Range – 400km/248.5 miles

T-62 Main Battle Tank

The T-62 was the next progression in the Soviet development cycle based on the T-54/55 series, and featured an enlarged hull to fit a new turret carrying a larger bore main gun. This tank was destined to become the primary main battle tank of the Soviet amoured forces during the 1970s, with over 20,000 built.

Weighing almost 40 tons, the T-62 was powered by the same 432.5kW/580hp V12 water-cooled diesel engine as its predecessor, which provided a top speed of 50kph/31.1mph and a range of 650km/403.9 miles. Mounted centrally over the third road wheel, the new "mushroom dome" cast turret had a U-5T (2A20) Rapira 115mm/4.53in main gun with a longer, thinner barrel than the 100mm/3.94in of the T-54/55. An unusual feature of the new turret was the automatic shell ejector system, which worked from the recoil of the main gun, ejecting the spent shell casings through a port in the rear of the turret.

There was also a 7.62mm/0.3in coaxial machine-gun and a 12.7mm/0.5in anti-aircraft machine-gun mounted by the loader's hatch. A gunner's infrared searchlight was mounted on the right, above the main gun. Later models included the usual improvements – gun stabilization and fire control, NBC

(Nuclear, Biological and Chemical) protection, communication and safety systems, add-on armour suites (including ERA (Explosive Reactive Armour), appliqué and increased belly armour for mine protection). Although there were many variations on the T-54/55 chassis, there were surprisingly few on the T-62, although the gun tank was upgraded regularly.

Recent modifications to various Marks of T-62 have included the fitting of some or all of the following: the Sheksna laser beam riding missile system; the Volna fire-control system, which includes the KDT-2 laser rangefinder with a range of 4,000m/13,123ft; a 12.7mm/0.5in AA machine-gun; a thermal sleeve for the barrel of the main gun; auxiliary armour to hull,

ABOVE, LEFT AND BELOW: **Using the T-55 as the basis for its design but with a longer, wider hull and a new turret, the T-62 came into Red Army service in 1961, but was first seen in public at the Moscow May Day Parade in 1965. Production continued until 1975, by which time over 20,000 had been built, including a wide family of variants. The 40,000kg/39.4-ton MBT had a crew of four and mounted a 115mm/4.53in smoothbore gun (40 rounds carried). Numerous modifications have been incorporated since it was accepted into service, including a flamethrower version.**

T-62 MBT

Entered service: 1961
Crew: 4
Weight: 40,000kg/39.4 tons
Dimensions: Length – 6.63m/21ft 9in
 Height (over turret hatch) – 2.39m/7ft 10in
 Width – 3.3m/10ft 10in
Armament: Main – 115mm/4.53in Rapira gun
 Secondary – 1 x 7.62mm/0.3in and
 1 x 12.7mm/0.5in machine-guns
Armour: Maximum – 242mm/9.53in
Powerplant: V55 12-cylinder diesel, delivering
 432.5kW/580hp
Performance: Speed – 50kph/31.1mph
 Range – 650km/403.9 miles (with additional fuel
 tank), 450km/280 miles (without)

turret and belly; ERA; side skirts; Napalm protection system; local smoke launchers; modernized suspension system; R-173 radio system; and V55U engine. The Sheksna missile, which is fired from the 115mm/4.53in gun, weighs some 28kg/61.72lb and has a range of 4,000m/13,123ft. Guidance is semi-automatic beam riding, so that all the operator has to do to ensure a hit is to keep the sight crosshairs on the target.

A conservative estimate of the number of T-62s built in the USSR and still in service worldwide is in excess of 8,000, spread among some 18 countries in Asia, the Middle and Far East, with North Korea having the largest holding (1,800) after Russia. Other T-62s were produced by the Czechs for export, while they were also once built in North Korea. The Russians are, therefore, currently offering a number of upgrades that will considerably improve the T-62's battlefield survivability.

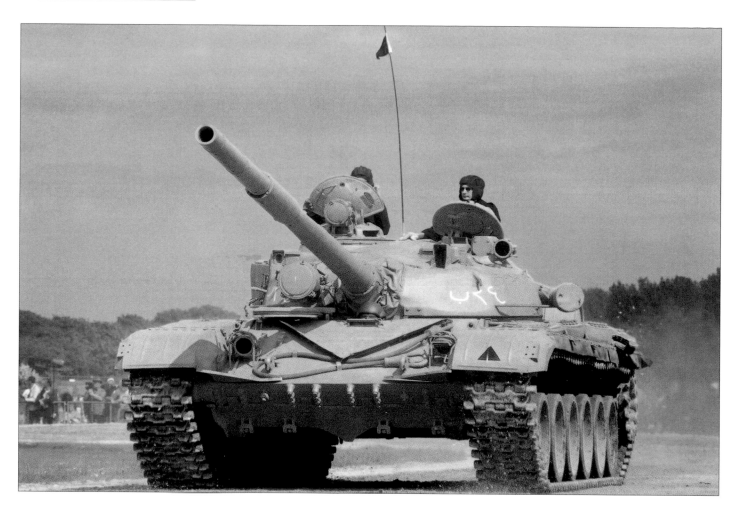

T-72 Main Battle Tank

Developed as an alternative to the highly complicated and expensive T-64 and introduced in 1972, the T-72 has a crew of three, weighs 45,500kg/44.8 tons and is powered by a V12 diesel engine, delivering a top speed of 60kph/37.3mph and a range of 550km/341.8 miles. The classic low, rounded turret is centred on the hull and has two cupolas, one each for the gunner and commander. The main armament is a stabilized 125mm/4.92in 2A46 smoothbore gun fitted with a light alloy thermal sleeve and served by an automatic carousel fitted vertically on the floor and attached to the rear wall of the turret, carrying 28 projectiles. This gun has the ability to fire both the Songster-type wire-guided missile as well as normal main gun

munitions. A 7.62mm/0.3in PKT machine-gun was also mounted coaxially to the right of the main armament and there was a 12.7mm/0.5in NSV machine-gun for anti-aircraft defence outside on the commander's cupola.

The tank also mounts a dozer blade under its nose, to clear obstacles and prepare fire positions, as well as having snorkelling equipment for deep wading. New versions had a cascade of improvements, including new engines (633.8kW/850hp, then 932.1kW/1,250hp), computerized fire-control systems, thermal and passive night-sights and fire detection and suppression systems. Variants included command, ARV, mine-clearer and bridgelayer models.

ABOVE AND LEFT: **Designed as a simpler alternative to the complicated and costly T-64, the T-72 has seen combat service in Iraq and Lebanon and is now serving with armies worldwide. Its main armament (on the T-72S) is the 125mm/4.92in smoothbore gun (45 rounds carried). The tank has recently been comprehensively upgraded and is in service with 30 different countries worldwide, the largest number (over 9,000) being in Russia. The T-72S weighs 1,000kg/2,204lb more than the T-72.**

ABOVE: **A captured Iraqi T-72 being dragged off during Operation "Desert Storm".** RIGHT: **During the 1970s the Soviets licensed the building of their T-72 to Yugoslavia, who adapted it to suit their own needs, putting in a different engine (a V12 diesel). Yugoslavia sold a number to Kuwait, and here are two of them, known as the M48A, flying Kuwaiti flags. These tanks saw combat during the first Gulf War.**

Like the T-54/55 series, the T-72 was built in massive numbers and supplied to client and satellite states, undergoing various modifications. They were also built under licence by seven other countries with their own model numbers, including the Czechoslovakian PSP T-72, the Polish PT-91 and the Yugoslavian M-84. There are even captured Arab-Israeli-modified versions.

RIGHT: **An internal view of part of the turret.** BELOW: **A T-72 with ERA on upgrade. The ERA bricks cover much of the vulnerable frontal area.**

T-72 MBT

Entered service: 1972
Crew: 3
Weight: 45,500kg/44.8 tons
Dimensions: Length – 9.53m/31ft 3in
Height (over turret hatch) – 2.22m/7ft 3in
Width – 3.59m/12ft 9in
Armament: Main – 125mm/4.92in gun
Secondary – 1 x 7.62mm/0.3in and
1 x 12.7mm/0.5in machine-guns
Armour: Maximum – 250mm/9.84in
Powerplant: V46 12-cylinder diesel, generating
581.6kW/780hp
Performance: Speed – 60kph/37.3mph
Range – 550km/341.8 miles (with long-range
tanks), 480km/300 miles (without)

LEFT: **Built both in Russia and the Ukraine, the T-64 MBT was the first Russian MBT to have a three-man crew, made possible by the installation of an automatic loader. The tank is only in service within armies of the Russian Federation and has never been offered for export.** BELOW: **Two T-64s being moved by tank train, a sensible way of preserving tank mileage. They are fitted with long-range fuel drums on the rear decks.** BOTTOM LEFT: **This T-64 MBT also has long-range fuel drums fitted above the rear engine deck. Its 125mm/4.92in smoothbore gun can fire the Songster ATGW (Anti-Tank Guided Weapon), taking 9–10 seconds to reach 4,000m/13,123ft.**

T-64 Main Battle Tank

Only ever in service with the Russian Federation and associate states, the T-64 MBT was never offered for export because it incorporated too many advanced features. The main differences between the T-64 and its predecessors were in its automotive and suspension systems, which consequently gave it a superior mobility. Weighing 42,000kg/41.3 tons, it was powered by a 5DTF 5-cylinder opposed-piston water-cooled diesel engine delivering a top speed of 75kph/46.6mph and a range of 400km/248.5 miles. Centred on the hull, the classic Soviet low-profile, rounded turret had two cupolas and mounted the 125mm/4.92in 2A26 Rapira 3 smoothbore main gun, fitted with a vertical ammunition stowage system and automatic loader, enabling the T-64 to be the first Soviet tank operated by a crew of three. There was also a 7.62mm/0.3in coaxial machine-gun mounted to the right of the mantlet and an infrared searchlight on the left of the main armament, as well as an optional 12.7mm/0.5in anti-aircraft machine-gun.

Other improvements included new armour to protect against HEAT (High-Explosive Anti-Tank) attack, incorporating conventional steel with ceramic inserts and called laminate, and also gill-type panels which sprung outward to detonate projectiles off the main body of the tank. As other models were introduced, the usual add-on armour suites also included ERA (Explosive Reactive Armour), passive and appliqué, as well as updates to the vehicle's gun stabilization and fire control, NBC (Nuclear, Biological and Chemical) protection, communication and safety systems. Variants included command, ARV (Armoured Recovery Vehicle) and Kobra missile-carrier models. Only about 8,000 T-64s were ever built, of which the largest number outside the Russian Federation are some 2,200 in service with the Ukrainian Army.

T-64 MBT

Entered service: 1972
Crew: 3
Weight: 42,000kg/41.3 tons
Dimensions: Length – 7.4m/24ft 3.5in
    Height (over turret hatch) – 2.2m/7ft 2.5in
    Width – 3.46m/11ft 4in
Armament: Main – 125mm/4.92in Rapira 3 gun
    Secondary – 1 x 7.62mm/0.3in and
    1 x 12.7mm/0.5in machine-guns
Armour: Maximum – 200mm/7.87in
Powerplant: 5DTF 5-cylinder diesel, 559.3kW/750hp
Performance: Speed – 75kph/46.6mph
    Range – 400km/248.5 miles

T-80 Main Battle Tank

The T-80 MBT was designed as an upgrade to replace the T-64, being produced at the Kirov Plant, Leningrad, and entering service in 1976. Initially only a small number were built and these were soon followed by the much improved T-80B.

Weighing 42,500kg/41.8 tons and fitted with torsion bar suspension, it was the first Soviet tank to have a gas-turbine engine – the GTD 1000 – which, coupled with a manual transmission, delivered a top speed of 70kph/43.5mph and a range of 335km/208.2 miles.

Unfortunately the engine proved a major stumbling block for the T-80, as it was very fuel-hungry and unreliable, necessitating changes to the hull shape in order to store more fuel as well as changes to the engine. The overall layout of the T-80 is similar to the T-64, but there are numerous differences in detail.

The wide flat turret is centred on the hull, with the commander's cupola on the right and the gunner's hatch on the left. It mounts a 125mm/4.92in 2A46 Rapira 3 smoothbore gun firing both ATGW (Anti-Tank Guided Weapon) missiles and normal main gun munitions, which is

served by a 28-projectile, horizontal automatic carousel loader, mounted on the floor and rear wall of the turret. A 7.62mm/0.3in coaxial machine-gun is mounted to the right of the mantlet and an infrared searchlight is mounted to the right of the main armament. The vehicle is also fitted with a dozer blade underneath the laminate armour glacis, as well as snorkelling equipment for deep wading.

The T-80B, which replaced the T-80 in 1978, had a modified up-armoured turret with an upgraded 125mm/4.92in main gun firing the new Kobra missile munition (known as Songster in US/NATO parlance) as well as a new fire-control system. Further upgrades include extensive extra frontal and ERA (Explosive, Reactive Armour) packages, a new, more powerful GTD-1250 turbine engine, a new laser-guided anti-tank main gun missile munition (Sniper), as well as an array of digital fire-control, navigation and safety systems.

Some 4,500 T-80s are in service in Russia, as well as a small number in four or five other countries, which surprisingly includes 41 in Cyprus.

TOP: **Similar to the T-64 series, the T-80 was accepted into service in 1976. It has a two-man turret and an automatic loader for its 125mm/4.92in smoothbore gun. A small number of T-80s have been purchased by Cyprus and Korea, as well as Pakistan, from the Ukraine factory. Note the large exhaust outlet at the rear.** ABOVE: **A Russian Federation T-80 firing on the ranges. It has a 125mm/4.92in 2A46M smoothbore gun, the same as that fitted to the T-72, and can fire either the Songster ATGW or 125mm/4.92in separate-loading ammunition (i.e. projectile-loaded first, then semi-combustible case, the stub base of which is the only part ejected).**

T-80 MBT

Entered service: 1976
Crew: 3
Weight: 42,500kg/41.8 tons
Dimensions: Length – 7.4m/24ft 3.5in
Height (over turret hatch) – 2.2m/7ft 2.5in
Width – 3.4m/11ft 2in
Armament: Main – 125mm/4.92in Rapira 3 gun
Secondary – 1 x 7.62mm/0.3in and
1 x 12.7mm/0.5in machine-guns
Armour: Unspecified
Powerplant: GTD 1000 12-cylinder gas-turbine,
820.3kW/1,100hp
Performance: Speed – 70kph/43.5mph
Range – 335km/208.2 miles

T-84 Main Battle Tank

The T-84 is a recent Ukrainian upgrade of the Russian T-80, with both being manufactured at the well-established Malyshev Plant at Kharkov in the Ukraine, and using as many locally produced components as possible. The main differences from its predecessor begin with a more powerful up-rated 6TD-2 diesel engine developing 894.8kW/1,200hp, which gave the vehicle a top speed of 65kph/40.4mph and a range of 540kph/335.5 miles. To handle this extra performance, new improved tracks were fitted.

Next, the turret mounted the Ukrainian-made 125mm/4.92in KBA3 smoothbore main gun, fitted with a

vertical carousel autoloader containing 28 rounds and an up-rated fire-control system including the French ALIS thermal sight. This armament fires both normal munitions and the Songster AT-11 Anti-Tank Guided Missile (ATGM).

Secondary armament consisted of two machine-guns – one of 7.62mm/ 0.3in and one of 12.7mm/0.5in. The T-84 also came equipped with an ARENA Active Protection System (APS) and the SHTORA-1 active IR (InfraRed) ATGM jammer – an electro-optical countermeasures system, along with Ukrainian-manufactured ERA (Explosive Reactive Armour) enhancements. Subsequent updates include improved

fire-control, communication, navigation and safety systems. There is also a later model mounting the NATO standard 120mm/4.72in main gun.

In 2001 the Ukrainian Army received two new T-84s – the first new main battle tanks delivered since the country became independent from Russia. As well as being accepted by the Ukrainian Army, this vehicle has been successfully sold to Pakistan and aroused the interest of other countries, including Turkey.

ABOVE AND LEFT: **Two views of the Ukranian-built T-84, some 8,000 having been built by the Malyshev plant for the Russian Army. Based upon the T-64 and designed jointly by the Leningrad Kirov plant and Malyshev, this MBT is now almost completely built in the Ukraine. It has a crew of three, weighs 46,000kg/45.3 tons and mounts a 125mm/4.92in smoothbore gun. These photographs were taken at an arms fair.**

T-84 MBT

Entered service: 1995
Crew: 3
Weight: 46,000kg/45.3 tons
Dimensions: Length – 7.08m/23ft 2.5in
 Height (over turret hatch) – 2.22m/7ft 3.5in
 Width – 3.56m/11ft 8in
Armament: Main – 125mm/4.92in KBA3 gun
 Secondary – 1 x 7.62mm/0.3in and
 1 x 12.7mm/0.5in machine-guns
Armour: Unspecified
Powerplant: 6TD-2 6-cylinder diesel, developing
 894.8kW/1,200hp
Performance: Speed – 65kph/40.4mph
 Range – 540km/335.5 miles

T-90 MBT

Entered service: 1993
Crew: 3
Weight: 46,500kg/45.8 tons
Dimensions: Length – 6.86m/22ft 6in
　　Height (over turret hatch) – 2.23m/7ft 4in
　　Width – 3.37m/11ft 1in
Armament: Main – 125mm/4.92in Rapira 3 gun
　　Secondary – 1 x 7.62mm/0.3in and
　　1 x 12.7mm/0.5in machine-guns
Armour: Unspecified
Powerplant: V-84MS 12-cylinder diesel,
　　626.4kW/840hp
Performance: Speed – 60kph/37.3mph
　　Range – 500km/310.7 miles

T-90 Main Battle Tank

The T-90 traces its development back to the T-72BM MBT – the improved T-72B with built-in ERA (Explosive Reactive Armour) – and was first manufactured at the Uralvagon Plant in Nizhnyi-Tagil in the late 1980s.

Developed at the same time as the T-80, but with a less complex and therefore cheaper design ethos, the first major difference between the two was in the choice of power pack, which in the T-90 was a V84MS diesel engine, producing 626.4kW/840hp and providing a top speed of 60kph/37.3mph and a range of 500km/310.7 miles.

The classic Russian low-profile, rounded turret is centred on the hull and mounts the 125mm/4.92in 2A46 smoothbore main gun (the same as the T-72 and T-80) firing the AT-11 Sniper laser-guided ATGM (Anti-Tank Guided Missile), as well as normal main gun munitions.

There is a coaxial 7.62mm/0.3in machine-gun and a 12.7mm/0.5in heavy anti-aircraft machine-gun on the turret top by the gunner's hatch. The T-90 also mounts two infrared searchlights on either side of the main armament, which are part of the Shtora ATGM defence system, and the turret is covered with second-generation ERA on the frontal arc, making this one of the best protected of Russian main battle tanks. It is equipped with the latest fire-control, navigation and safety systems. There is also a T-90S MBT version, designed to meet the operational requirements of Asian countries – some 310 having been bought by India.

TOP AND ABOVE: **The T-90, which is yet another development of the T-72, first came to prominence in 1993 and is believed to have gone into small-scale production the following year. It has a crew of three, with a two-man turret with an automatic loader for its 125mm/4.92in gun. The photographs show a snorkel attached to the turret rear, but no long-range fuel tanks fitted on the rear. It made its first appearance outside Russia at Abu Dhabi in March 1997.** LEFT: **Standard equipment on the T-90S is the latest generation of Kontakt 5 Explosive Reactive Armour, as fitted in this photograph.**

TR-580 and TR-85 Main Battle Tanks

Both the TR-580 and TR-85 are Romanian variants of the Russian T-55 series, manufactured or modified at the Brashove factory in Romania, and the prime weapon of their armoured forces in the 1980s and 1990s.

The TR-580 was the first redesign, its alphanumeric name denoting the size of its 432.5kW/580hp engine, which necessitated a hull redesign. It was armed with the same weapons as the T-55 and its sister vehicle the TR-85, and weighed over 37 tons. It was fitted with a new torsion bar suspension system, the main visual difference between both of the Romanian vehicles and their T-55 predecessor being the sixth road wheel (the T-55 only had five).

The TR-85 also has a new German 641.3kW/860hp 8-cylinder diesel engine, providing a top speed of 60kph/38mph and a range of 310km/192.6 miles,

which required substantial modification of the rear hull and decking. In the turret the main armament mounted was the same 100mm/3.94in gun with a new fire-control system and two machine-guns – one of 7.62mm/0.3in and one of 12.7mm/0.5in.

One visual difference between the two tanks is the spoked road wheels of the TR-580. An upgrade currently under development ports additional passive armour, a new fire-control and gun-stabilization system, as well as night-vision and safety equipment updates.

LEFT: The Romanian TR-85 MBT is a local Romanian design which is very similar to the Russian T-55. In the early 1990s the Romanians said that they had over 600 of these MBTs in service, but that figure has now dropped. The TR-85 is basically a T-55 with a fume extractor fitted to the end of the 100mm/ 3.94in rifled main armament and a thermal sleeve. There is also an upgrade mooted which has a new power pack (596.6kW/800hp diesel) and a fully automatic transmission. The TR-85M1 is the upgraded version of the TR-85, built in the 1970s with German help in chassis technology, the prime Romanian contractor being Arsenalul Armetel. Various foreign companies were also involved.

TR-85 MBT

Entered service: 1987
Crew: 4
Weight: 50,000kg/49.2 tons
Dimensions: Length – 9.96m/32ft 8in
  Height (over turret hatch) – 3.10m/10ft 2in
  Width – 3.44m/11ft 3.5in
Armament: Main – 100mm/3.94in gun
  Secondary – 1 x 7.62mm/0.3in and
  1 x 12.7mm/0.5in machine-guns
Armour: Unspecified
Powerplant: MTU 8-cylinder diesel,
  641.3kW/860hp
Performance: Speed – 60kph/37.3mph
  Range – 310km/192.6 miles

RIGHT: The other Romanian MBT is the TR-580, which is very similar to the TR-85 that it preceded in production. The main differences are that the gun does not have a thermal sleeve or laser rangefinder installed.

TR-580 MBT

Entered service: 1982
Crew: 4
Weight: 38,200kg/37.6 tons
Dimensions: Length – 6.45m/21ft 2in
  Height (over turret hatch) – 2.4m/7ft 10.5in
  Width – 3.27m/10ft 8.5in
Armament: Main – 100mm/3.94in gun
  Secondary – 1 x 7.62mm/0.3in and
  1 x 12.7mm/0.5in machine-guns
Armour: Unspecified
Powerplant: Thought to be 12-cylinder diesel,
  432.5kW/580hp
Performance: Speed – 60kph/37.3mph
  Range – 300km/186.4 miles

LEFT: Based upon the T-72, the TR-125 MBT is heavier (48,000kg/47.2 tons), with thicker armour and a larger engine. It can be recognized externally from the additional seventh roadwheel on either side. Armament is identical to the T-72.

TR-125 MBT

Entered service: 1989
Crew: 4
Weight: 48,000kg/47.2 tons
Dimensions: Length – 6.9m/22ft 7.5in
    Height (over turret hatch) – 2.37m/7ft 9.5in
    Width – 3.60m/11ft 9.5in
Armament: Main – 125mm/4.92in gun
    Secondary – 1 x 7.62mm/0.3in and
    1 x 12.7mm/0.5in machine-guns
Armour: Unspecified
Powerplant: V12 diesel, 656.2kW/880hp
Performance: Speed – 60kph/37.3mph
    Range – 540km/335.5 miles

TR-125 Main Battle Tank

The TR-125 is a Romanian-built version of the Soviet T-72, manufactured at the end of the 1980s until the collapse of the USSR led to the cessation of production in favour of other vehicles. With considerably thicker armour, it was heavier than its predecessor, weighing 48,000kg/ 47.2 tons, with a crew of four. The TR-125 was powered by a V12 diesel engine, providing a top speed of 60kph/ 37.3mph and a range of 540km/335.5 miles. It was armed with a 125mm/4.92in main gun, with a coaxial 7.62mm/0.3in machine-gun and one of 12.7mm/ 0.5in for anti-aircraft defence. The main visual difference between it and other T-72 variants is in it having a seventh road wheel. It is still in service with the Romanian Army today.

TM-800 Main Battle Tank

The most recent of the Romanian-manufactured MBTs, the TM-800 first emerged in the mid-1990s as an upgraded version of the TR-580 – itself a T-55 derivative. With new laminate armour increasing its weight to 45,000kg/44.3 tons but giving it improved survivability on the battlefield, and powered by its 618.9kW/830hp diesel engine, the TM-800 has a top speed of 60kph/37.3mph and a range of 500km/310.7 miles. In its "mushroom head" two-hatched turret it mounts a 100mm/3.94in D10 series main gun with a computerized fire-control system and laser rangefinder, along with two machine-guns – one an internal coaxial of 7.62mm/0.3in and the other a heavier calibre 12.7mm/0.5in mounted on the outside of the turret for anti-aircraft (AA) defence.

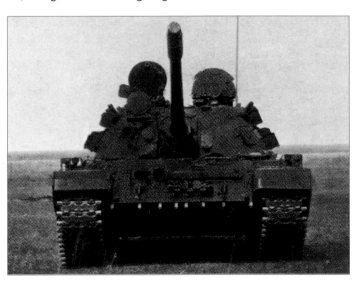

LEFT: The TM-800 is an up-rated TR-580 MBT, currently the most modern Romanian MBT. It appeared in service in 1994 and has not yet gone into full production.

TM-800 MBT

Entered service: 1994
Crew: 4
Weight: 45,000kg/44.3 tons
Dimensions: Length – 6.74m/22ft 1.5in
    Height (over turret hatch) – 2.35m/7ft 8.5in
    Width – 3.30m/10ft 10in
Armament: Main – 100mm/3.94in gun
    Secondary – 1 x 7.62mm/0.3in and
    1 x 12.7mm/0.5in machine-guns
Armour: Unspecified
Powerplant: Diesel, 618.9kW/830hp
Performance: Speed – 60kph/37.3mph
    Range – 500km/310.7 miles

LEFT: **In the early 1950s the Soviet Union supplied China with a number of their T-54 Main Battle Tanks and afterwards, production of such MBTs was taken on by NORINCO (China North Industries Corporation) under the designation of Type 59. Later Type 59As were fitted with an IR searchlight above the 100mm/3.94in gun, while other retrofits have included a more powerful diesel and even an RO Defence 105mm/4.13in L7A3 rifled gun to improve the resulting package.** BELOW: **This Type 59 has been fitted with the British 105mm/4.13in L7A3 rifled gun, a private venture by UK Royal Ordnance (now BAe Systems). Note also the British pattern smoke dischargers.** BOTTOM: **A column of parked Chinese Type 59-IIs. They were a further development of the Type 59, and also had a number of improvements, such as stabilization for the main gun, a 432.5kW/580hp diesel engine and new radios.**

Type 59 Main Battle Tank

The Chinese Type 59 and its successor the Type 69 were both based upon the Soviet T-54 and it was the first Chinese tank built under licence at the inception of its own permanent armoured formations. With an identical layout to its Soviet predecessor, manned by the same number of crew and weighing 36,000kg/35.4 tons, its V12 diesel engine gave it a top speed of 50kph/31.1mph and a range of 420km/ 261 miles. Within its classic Russian "mushroom head" turret, it mounted a 100mm/3.94in rifled gun, together with two coaxial machine-guns, plus a 12.7mm/0.5in on top for anti-aircraft

defence. At first the Type 59 had only the bare essentials, but later models have mounted infrared searchlights, laser rangefinders, night-vision equipment and armour enhancements.

Both Type 59s and Type 69s have been built in large numbers for the People's Liberation Army and for export, an estimate being that some 6,000 are still in service in China, while it has been sold to over a dozen countries,

one of the largest numbers being about 1,200 in Pakistan, which now produces them locally and has exported to other countries in Asia and Africa.

Type 59 MBT	
Entered service: 1959	
Crew: 4	
Weight: 36,000kg/35.4 tons	
Dimensions: Length – 7.9m/25ft 11in	
Height (over turret hatch) – 2.59m/8ft 6in	
Width – 3.27m/10ft 8.5in	
Armament: Main – 100mm/3.94in gun	
Secondary – 2 x 7.62mm/0.3in and	
1 x 12.7mm/0.5in machine-guns	
Armour: Maximum – 203mm/7.99in	
Powerplant: 12150L V12 diesel, generating 320.7kW/430hp	
Performance: Speed – 50kph/31.1mph	
Range – 420km/262.5 miles	

Type 61 Main Battle Tank

Japan's first post-World War II attempt at MBT construction, The Type 61 emerged in 1962 after a development phase of almost a decade, looking very like the M48 Patton that it was so obviously based on.

Built using welded rolled steel and with a cast turret, the vehicle weighed 35,000kg/34.4 tons and was fitted with torsion bar suspension. It had a crew of four, and was powered by a Mitsubishi Type 12 HM 21 WT diesel engine delivering a top speed of 45kph/28mph and a range of 200km/124.3 miles. Mounted in the dome-shaped turret with its bulging rear was a newly designed

Type 61 90mm/3.54in main gun which was not fitted with stabilization and therefore could not fire accurately on the move. There were two machine-guns – one 7.62mm/0.3in internal coaxial and the other of 12.7mm/0.5in for anti-aircraft defence.

There were also an ARV (Armoured Recovery Vehicle), AVLB (Armoured Vehicle Launched Bridge), Armoured Engineer and a Type 61 training tank.

Although it never saw action anywhere and was only in service with the Japanese Defence Force, it proved an important step in the return to indigenous tank production for the Japanese.

TOP AND ABOVE: **The first Japanese-built tank after World War II, the Type 61 was heavily influenced by the Americans. Over 500 were built of this 35,000kg/34.4-ton four-man MBT, which was armed with a 90mm/3.54in gun.**

LEFT: **Japan did not take much interest in tanks during World War II, so the Type 61 gave them a great deal of useful experience. Although it resembled the M48, it had no stabilization on its main armament. A small number are still in service.**

Type 61 MBT

Entered service: 1962
Crew: 4
Weight: 35,000kg/34.4 tons
Dimensions: Length – 8.19m/26ft 10.5in
   Height (over turret hatch) – 2.49m/8ft 2in
   Width – 2.95m/9ft 8in
Armament: Main – 90mm/3.54in Type 61 gun
   Secondary – 1 x 7.62mm/0.3in and
   1 x 12.7mm/0.5in machine-guns
Armour: Maximum – 64mm/2.52in
Powerplant: Mitsubishi HM21WT diesel,
   447.4kW/600hp
Performance: Speed – 45kph/28mph
   Range – 200km/124.3 miles

LEFT: **The Type 62 Light Tank was a reduced-size version of their Type 59 MBT, which was a licensed copy of the Red Army T-59. It was the first "home-grown" light tank in Chinese service. Some 800 were built, and many still serve in training units.**

Type 62 Light Tank

Entered service: China
Crew: 4
Weight: 21,000kg/20.7 tons
Dimensions: Length – 7.9m/25ft 11in (gun forward)
  Height (over turret hatch) – 2.25m/7ft 4.5in
  Width – 2.68m/8ft 9.5in
Armament: Main – 85mm/3.35in gun
  Secondary – 2 x 7.62mm/0.3in and
  1 x 12.7mm/0.5in machine-guns
Armour: Unspecified
Powerplant: Thought to be 12-cylinder diesel,
  320.7kW/430hp
Performance: Speed – 60kph/37.3mph
  Range – 500km/310.7 miles

Type 62 Light Tank

The Type 62 Chinese Light Tank is based on the previous Type 59 and was introduced in 1962 as an indigenous scaled-down version of its predecessor with a much lower ground pressure to cope with the specific environments of rough and soft terrain. Weighing 21,000kg/20.7 tons and with a crew of four, the Type 62 was powered by a 320.7kW/430hp diesel engine providing a top speed of 60kph/37.3mph and a range of 500km/310.7 miles. In its Russian-style "mushroom head" turret it mounted an 85mm/3.35in rifled main gun, along with a coaxial 7.62mm/0.3in machine-gun, and another of 12.7mm/0.5in for anti-aircraft defence located by the loader's hatch. There was also another 7.62mm/0.3in machine-gun in the bow operated by the driver. Approximately 800 are currently in Chinese service, and this AFV was widely exported to countries in Africa and Asia, especially Vietnam. The vehicle has been modified into ARV (Armoured Recovery Vehicle) and engineering variants, and there is also a tropicalized version.

Type 63 Light Amphibious Tank

The Type 63 is a light tank with amphibious capability and is of a similar size and weight to the Type 62. It also shares its turret and weapons systems, although its hull is based on the Type 77 APC. With a weight of over 18 tons, the Type 63 is powered by a 12150 LV12 diesel engine, giving a top speed of 64kph/39.8mph and a range of 370km/229.9 miles. Propulsion in the water is provided by hyrdo-jets located at the hull rear. It is estimated that some 1,200 are in service with the Chinese Army and Marine Corps, at least 500 of which have been upgraded to Type 63A standard, carrying a large three-man turret armed with a 105mm/4.13in rifled main gun. It is also in service with North Korea, Myanmar (Burma) and Vietnam.

RIGHT: **The Type 63 was the Chinese improvement on the Red Army PT-76 Light Amphibious Tank, which combined the T-54/T-55 turret on to the Type 77 APC chassis. It will most probably be replaced by the Type 99 Light Tank when it comes into full production.**

Type 63 Light Amphibious Tank

Entered service: 1963
Crew: 4
Weight: 18,400kg/18.1 tons
Dimensions: Length – 8.44m/27ft 8.5in
  Height (over turret hatch) – 2.52m/8ft 3.5in
  Width – 3.2m/10ft 6in
Armament: Main – 85mm/3.35in gun
  Secondary – 1 x 7.62mm/0.3in and
  1 x 12.7mm/0.5in machine-guns
Armour: Maximum – 14mm/0.55in
Powerplant: 12150LV 12-cylinder diesel,
  298.3kW/400hp
Performance: Speed – 64kph/39.8mph
  Range – 370km/229.9 miles

Type 69 Main Battle Tank

The first firm sighting of a Type 69 was on a Beijing parade in 1982. It entered service earlier – perhaps even as early as 1969, hence its name. Although it looks much like its predecessor, the Type 59, it has had a whole raft of new fire-control, stabilization, NBC (Nuclear, Biological and Chemical) protection, navigation and safety systems installed. At one time British Royal Ordnance produced a Type 59 armed with a 105mm/4.13in L7 series rifled gun for the export market. The Type 69-I MBT is now armed with a 100mm/3.94in smoothbore gun, while the Type 69-II MBT has a 105mm/4.13in rifled gun (possibly derived from the L7) and fitted with a thermal sleeve. There are also command, ARV (Armoured Recovery Vehicle), mine-clearing and twin 57mm/2.24in anti-aircraft variants.

BELOW: **These Type 69s are in Iraqi desert livery, having been captured by Coalition forces in the first Gulf War. Note the large 12.7mm/0.5in heavy anti-aircraft machine-gun on the top of the turret of the nearest one.**

TOP: **Two Chinese Type 69-IIs (sold to Pakistan) on parade with the Pakistan Army. Note that they have been upgraded by fitting the 105mm/4.13in gun.** ABOVE: **Captured by Coalition forces during the first Gulf War, this Type 69-II has lost its laser rangefinder, which is usually externally mounted over the main armament.**

Type 69 MBT

Entered service: 1980 (or perhaps as early as 1969)
Crew: 4
Weight: 36,700kg/36.1 tons
Dimensions: Length – 6.24m/20ft 5.5in
   Height (over turret hatch) – 2.81m/9ft 2.5in
   Width – 3.3m/10ft 10in
Armament: Main – 100mm/3.94in gun
   Secondary – 2 x 7.62mm/0.3in and
   1 x 12.7mm/0.5in machine-guns
Armour: Maximum – 100mm/3.94in
Powerplant: 1210L-7BW V12 diesel,
   432.5kW/580hp
Performance: Speed – 50kph/31.1mph
   Range – 420km/261 miles

Type 74 Main Battle Tank

The Type 74 MBT was the next tank developed and produced by Japan to succeed the Type 61. Having tested two different prototypes – the primary difference between them being manual or automatic loading of the main gun – the manual version was chosen, with the vehicle being produced by Mitsubishi Heavy Industries and first appearing in 1975. Weighing 38,000kg/37.4 tons and fitted with a new vertically variable hydro-pneumatic suspension system, the Type 74 is powered by a Mitsubishi 10ZF22 WT 10-cylinder diesel engine, providing a top speed of 60kph/37.3mph and a range of 400km/248.5 miles. In the electrically powered turret – a sleeker looking version of the M47/48, but still with a rear bulge – the main armament is the British-designed 105mm/4.13in L7 type rifled tank gun, manufactured under licence in Japan. There is also one 7.62mm/0.3in coaxial machine-gun and one of 12.7mm/0.5in for Anti-Aircraft (AA) and close-quarter defence. Internally the vehicle is equipped with all the latest target and fire

ABOVE AND BELOW LEFT: **Designed by Mitsubishi in the early 1960s, the Type 74 was completed in 1969 when it was known as the STB 1. However, it was not until 1973 that the final production model was completed. Another two more years elapsed before the production run of some 560 were built and it replaced the Type 61.**

control, gun stabilization, NBC (Nuclear, Biological and Chemical) protection, communication, navigation, night-vision and safety systems. Variants include an ARV (Armoured Recovery Vehicle) and a twin 35mm/1.38in AA gun version. Approximately 560 were built, but all have now been phased out of front-line service.

Type 74 MBT

Entered service: 1975
Crew: 4
Weight: 38,000kg/37.4 tons
Dimensions: Length – 9.42m/30ft 11in
    Height (over turret hatch) – 2.48m/8ft 1.5in
    Width – 3.18m/10ft 5in
Armament: Main – 105mm/4.13in L7 gun
    Secondary – 1 x 7.62mm/0.3in and
    1 x 12.7mm/0.5in machine-guns
Armour: Unspecified
Powerplant: Mitsubishi 10ZF22 WT 10-cylinder
    diesel, 536.9kW/720hp
Performance: Speed – 60kph/37.3mph
    Range – 400km/248.5 miles

LEFT: The Type 80 became famous (or should it be infamous?) with the well-publicized scenes of crushing the students' revolt in Tiananmen Square. The Type 80 was a major advance in Chinese tank design, incorporating many new developments such as stabilization and a computerized fire-controlled system. BELOW: This Type 80 is showing off its ability to negotiate a sizeable vertical obstacle. To extend its operational range, it could be fitted with two large fuel drums at the rear (not fitted here) which could be jettisoned after use. BOTTOM: This immaculately painted Type 80-II was photographed in Beijing, probably during a military parade.

Type 80 Main Battle Tank

Development of the Chinese Type 80 MBT began in the early 1980s, and full production was achieved towards the end of that decade. Although based on the Type 59/69 series, it has a newly designed chassis and running gear, with six road wheels and a torsion bar suspension system. Weighing 38,500kg/ 37.9 tons and with a crew of four, the Type 80 is powered by a VR36 V12 diesel engine, providing a top speed of 60kph/ 37.3mph and a range of 430km/267.2 miles. The turret has a "mushroom head" profile similar to the Type 69 but with a distinctive open grill stowage basket wrapped around the back and sides.

The main armament is an L7 type 105mm/4.13in rifled main gun fitted with a fume extractor and a thermal sleeve. There is also a coaxial 7.62mm/0.3in machine-gun and a 12.7mm/0.5in anti-aircraft machine-gun mounted outside the loader's hatch. The Type 80 ports all the latest essential equipment, including a ballistics computer, a laser rangefinder integrated with stabilized sights, attack sensors and composite armour suites. To extend the operational range of the Type 80 MBT, two large drum fuel tanks (jettisonable) can be fitted at the rear.

Some 500 Type 80 Main Battle Tanks are in service with the Chinese army and a small number were exported to Myanmar (Burma).

Type 80 MBT	

Entered service: 1988
Crew: 4
Weight: 38,500kg/37.9 tons
Dimensions: Length – 9.33m/30ft 7.5in
   Height (over turret hatch) – 2.29m/7ft 6in
   Width – 3.37m/11ft 0.5in
Armament: Main – 105mm/4.13in gun
   Secondary – 1 x 7.62mm/0.3in and
   1 x 12.7mm/0.5in machine-guns
Armour: Unspecified
Powerplant: VR36 V12 diesel, 544.4kW/730hp
Performance: Speed – 60kph/37.3mph
   Range – 430km/267.2 miles

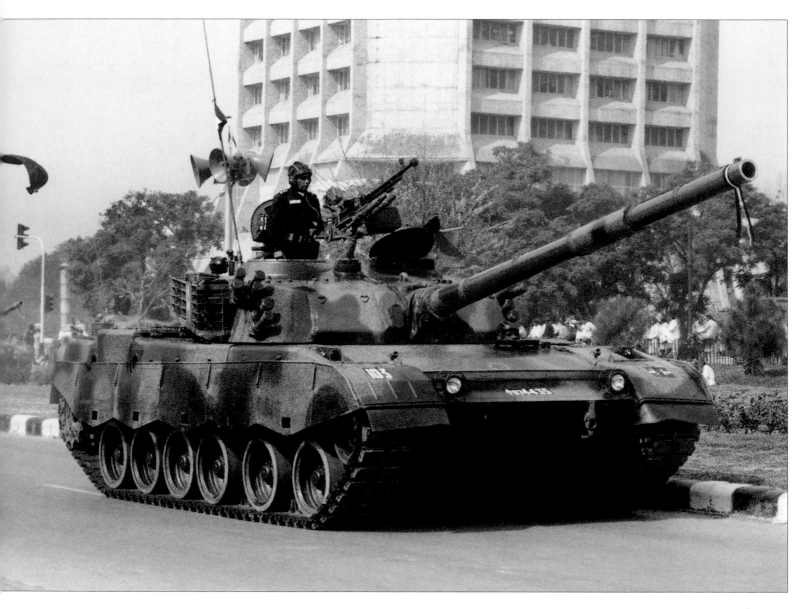

Type 85-II Main Battle Tank

The Type 85-II Chinese MBT is an upgrade of the Type 80 with an improved chassis and a new, flatter welded turret, using the latest upgraded modular composite armour. Weighing just over 40 tons, it is powered by a V12 supercharged diesel engine, giving it a top speed of 62kph/39mph and a range of 450km/280 miles. Initially it mounted the same 105mm/4.13in main armament as its predecessor, but this has recently been upgraded to a larger, fully stabilized 125mm/4.92in smoothbore main gun served by an autoloader, thus reducing the crew to three. This weapon enables the Type 85 to fire accurately on the move – the first Chinese MBT to be able do so, which is a significant advantage.

ABOVE: **The Type 85-II initially had a 105mm/4.13in rifled gun, which has now been replaced by a 125mm/4.92in smoothbore gun with an automatic loader. In recent years China has exported more than 250 to Pakistan – known as the Type 85-IIAP, which is shown in this photograph.**

The most recent version, the Type 85-III is in service with the Chinese army and is built under licence in Pakistan, where its nomenclature is the Type 85-IIAP.

Variants

The Type 85-IIM, known in the People's Liberation Army as the Type 88C MBT, was first seen in 1999. It weighs 41,000kg/ 40.35 tons and is armoured with an automatic loader. It has the ISFCS 22 computerized fire-control system fitted. Some also appear to have been fitted with a laser-jamming device operated from inside the turret and mounted on the left side of the turret roof.

Type 85-II MBT

Entered service: 1995
Crew: 3
Weight: 41,000kg/40.35 tons
Dimensions: Length – 10.1m/33ft 1.5in
  Height (over turret hatch) – 2.37m/7ft 9.5in
  Width – 3.50m/11ft 6in
Armament: Main – 125mm/4.92in gun
  Secondary – 1 x 7.62mm/0.3in and
  1 x 12.7mm/0.5in machine-guns
Armour: Unspecified
Powerplant: Perkins V12 diesel, 894.8kW/1,200hp
Performance: Speed – 62kph/38.5mph
  Range – 450km/279.6 miles

Type 88 K1 Main Battle Tank

Emerging in 1987 from a joint US–South Korean project begun in 1980, the Type 88 K1/K1A1 MBT is now entirely South Korean-built, with various parts manufactured under licence. It resembles the Abrams in appearance, with its flat faceted composite armoured turret. Weighing 51,100kg/50.3 tons and fitted with a hybrid suspension system combining hydro-pneumatic elements and torsion bar springs, the Type 88 K1 is powered by an MTU MB 871 Ka-501 turbocharged diesel engine, giving a top speed of 65kph/40.4mph and a range of 440km/273.4 miles.

Main armament in earlier models was the same as the M1, the 105mm/4.13in gun, along with three machine-guns, two of 7.62mm/0.3in and one of 12.7mm/ 0.5in. However, the latest version, the K1A1, mounts the M1A1's 120mm/4.72in smoothbore main gun. The vehicle also ports the latest target and fire control, gun stabilization, NBC (Nuclear,

Biological and Chemical) protection, communication, navigation, night-vision and safety systems.

There are also up-armour packages as well as ARV (Armoured Recovery Vehicle), mine-clearing vehicle and bridge-layer variants, all of which are currently being marketed to other countries, but to date without success.

TOP: **In early 1980 the Republic of South Korea chose the General Dynamics Company of the United States to design and build a new main battle tank for them. A few years later the Type 88 K1 appeared, which looks very like the Abrams M1 and mounts the same 105mm/4.13in gun.**

ABOVE: **Over 1,000 K1s have been built by Hyundai for the South Korean Army. Future developments may include a lighter model, that would include fitting ERA, to sell to other Far Eastern armies.**

Type 88 K1 MBT	

Entered service: 1987
Crew: 4
Weight: 51,100kg/50.3 tons
Dimensions: Length – 7.48m/24ft 6.5in
   Height (over turret hatch) – 2.25m/7ft 4.5in
   Width – 3.59m/11ft 9.5in
Armament: Main – 105mm/4.13in gun
   Secondary – 2 x 7.62mm/0.3in and
   1 x 12.7mm/0.5in machine-guns
Armour: Unspecified
Powerplant: MTU MB 871 Ka-501 diesel,
   984.8kW/1,200hp
Performance: Speed – 65kph/40.4mph
   Range – 440km/273.4 miles

119

Type 90 Main Battle Tank

In 1976, development of the next indigenous Japanese tank was initiated as soon as the Type 74 had entered service and, in 1990, the Type 90 was produced by a consortium of Japanese companies headed by Mitsubushi Heavy Industries. Weighing 50,000kg/49.2 tons and fitted with a hybrid hydro-pneumatic and torsion bar suspension system, the Type 90 is powered by a Mitsubishi 10ZG 10-cylinder liquid-cooled diesel engine, giving it a speed of 70kph/43.5mph and a range of 400km/248.5 miles. The German Rheinmetall 120mm/4.72in smoothbore

main gun – the same armament as Leopard 2 – is mounted in a wide, flat turret resembling that of the Abrams M1A1 and is armoured with a combination of the latest composite and laminate packages. This weapon was chosen after extensive testing in preference over the original Japanese design, and it is served by an autoloader, thereby reducing the crew to three.

Secondary weaponry includes the normal 7.62mm/0.3in coaxial and 12.7mm/0.5in machine-guns. The vehicle is also equipped with the latest digital fire-control,

ABOVE AND BELOW LEFT: **Mitsubishi was the prime contractor for this Japanese MBT that was first designed in 1976. Apart from its 120mm/4.72in smoothbore Rheinmetall gun, it was completely Japanese-designed and built. Later, two prototypes with Japanese 120mm/4.72in guns (firing Japanese ammunition) were also built. It is now in service with the Japanese Ground Self-Defence Force, and has never been offered on the export market.**

navigation, night-vision, communication and safety systems. The Type 90 is currently in Japanese service but has not been offered for export. There are the usual ARV (Armoured Recovery Vehicle), AVLB (Armoured Vehicle Launched Bridge) and mine-clearing variants.

Type 90 MBT	

Entered service: 1991
Crew: 3
Weight: 50,000kg/49.2 tons
Dimensions: Length – 9.76m/32ft
  Height (over turret hatch) – 2.34m/7ft 8in
  Width – 3.43m/11ft 3in
Armament: Main – 120mm/4.72in gun
  Secondary – 1 x 7.62mm/0.3in and
  1 x 12.7mm/0.5in machine-guns
Armour: Unspecified
Powerplant: Mitsubishi 10ZG 10-cylinder diesel,
  1,118.6kW/1,500hp
Performance: Speed – 70kph/43.5mph
  Range – 400km/248.5 miles

Type 90-II (MBT 2000) Main Battle Tank

The NORINCO Type 90-II MBT, also now known as MBT 2000, first emerged in 1991 and was a development of the Type 85 design, with the first model never reaching production stage. Having undergone armour, engine and main gun upgrades, the new improved model, Type 90-II, weighed over 47 tons and was powered by a Perkins V12 diesel engine, providing a top speed of 62kph/38.5mph and a range of 450km/279.6 miles. Mounted in a flat turret tapering at the front and fitted with a kind of composite armour, the 125mm/4.92in smoothbore main gun is served by an automatic loader, allowing the tank to be crewed by three men – commander, gunner and driver. Secondary armament consists of two machine-guns – one of 7.62mm/0.3in and one of 12.7mm/0.5in.

Internally, the digital fire-control system includes a stabilized laser rangefinder sight, passive thermal imaging and crosswind, tilt and angular velocity sensors, allowing the Type 90-II to engage targets accurately while on the move in day or night conditions.

Currently in Chinese service, this AFV has been marketed for export under the name of MBT 2000 and, following a further agreement, Pakistan has been licensed to produce the Type 90-II, renaming it the Al-Khalid.

LEFT: **The Type 90 appeared in the early 1990s, and had considerable improvements in firepower, protection and mobility over previous Chinese MBTs. The main armament of this 48,000kg/ 47.2-ton three-man tank is a 125mm/4.92in smoothbore gun with an automatic loader and Image Stabilized Fire-Control System. Additional fuel drums can be mounted on the rear.**

Type 90-II (MBT 2000) MBT

Entered service: 1995
Crew: 3
Weight: 48,000kg/47.2 tons
Dimensions: Length – 10.1m/33ft 1.5in
　　Height (over turret hatch) – 2.37m/7ft 9.5in
　　Width – 3.50m/11ft 6in
Armament: Main – 125mm/4.92in gun
　　Secondary – 1 x 7.62mm/0.3in and
　　1 x 12.7mm/0.5in machine-guns
Armour: Unspecified
Powerplant: Perkins V12 diesel, generating
　　894.8kW/1,200hp
Performance: Speed – 62kph/38.5mph
　　Range – 450km/279.6 miles

Type 98 Main Battle Tank

A little-seen upgrade development of the Type 90-II is the Type 98 MBT, first glimpsed in 1999 at the 50th Anniversary of the Chinese People's Republic. It is an upgrade of the Type 90-II, with the same armament mounted on a modified turret with a new modular armour package. Improvements will no doubt include substantial enhancement of its fire-control, navigation, NBC (Nuclear, Biological and Chemical) protection and safety systems. It is currently in production and has been deployed with the People's Liberation Army (PLA).

Development is continuing, and an improved Type 98 with a heavier combat weight (52,800kg/52 tons) has appeared. It retains the 125mm/4.92in smoothbore main gun and is said to be more reliable and better protected, possibly using the "arrowhead"-type armour as on the latest Leopard 2.

Type 98 MBT

Entered service: 1998
Crew: 35
Weight: 50,793kg/50 tons
Dimensions: Length – 11m/36ft
　　Height (over turret hatch) – approximately 2m/6ft 6in
　　Width – 3.4m/11ft 2in
Armament: Main – 125mm/4.92in gun
　　Secondary – 1 x 7.62mm/0.3in and
　　1 x 12.7mm/0.5in machine-guns
Armour: Not known
Powerplant: 894.8kW/1,200hp diesel
Performance: Speed – 65kph/40.6mph
　　Range – 450km/280 miles (600km/375 miles with
　　external fuel tanks)

LEFT: **Yet another parade and another immaculate Chinese tank, this time a Type 98, one of their most modern tanks, clearly showing its 125mm/4.92in smoothbore gun.**

Vickers Mark 1 (Vijayanta) Main Battle Tank

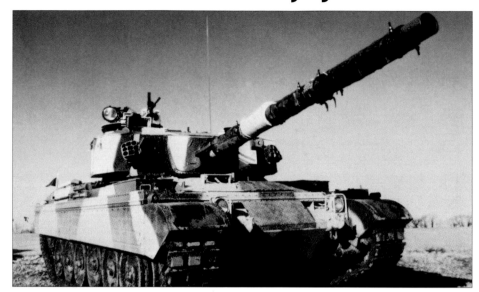

LEFT: **It was in the late 1950s that Vickers began to consider producing a tank to its own design for overseas markets. First to be produced was the Mark 1 MBT which weighed 38,600kg/38 tons, had a crew of four and mounted a 105mm/4.13in gun. A total of 70 Mark 1s were sold to Kuwait.**

Vickers Mark 1 (Vijayanta) MBT

Entered service: 1964
Crew: 4
Weight: 40,400kg/39.77 tons
Dimensions: Length – 7.92m/26ft
  Height (over turret hatch) – 2.44m/8ft
  Width – 3.17m/10ft 5in
Armament: Main – 105mm/4.13in L7 gun
  Secondary – 2 x 7.62mm/0.3in and
  1 x 12.7mm/0.5in machine-guns
Armour: Maximum – 80mm/3.15in
Powerplant: Leyland L60 6-cylinder multi-fuel,
  484.7kW/650bhp
Performance: Speed – 48kph/29.8mph
  Range – 480km/298.3 miles

The Vickers Mark 1 was based on the Chieftain MBT but produced in a lightly armoured configuration in 1964 for the Asian and Arab export market. This was a viable AFV, if not of NATO MBT quality, and was built using as many existing parts as possible. Weighing 38,600kg/38 tons, it was powered by a Leyland L60 Mk 4B 6-cylinder water-cooled multi-fuel engine which provided a top speed of 48kph/29.8mph and a range of 480km/298.3 miles. It was armed with the Royal Ordnance L7 105mm/4.13in main gun as well as two 7.62mm/0.3in and one 12.7mm/0.5in machine-guns. These were mounted in a turret that resembled the Centurion's in appearance, having an angular flat box shape with a rear stowage bustle, rather than the Chieftain's more ergonomic turret shape. The main customer of the Vickers Mark 1 was India, where a prototype had been sent in 1963. Accepted by India, it was renamed the Vijayanta (Victory), and local production was started in 1965 by an Vickers Indian subsidiary in Madras.

Local modifications were made over the years that followed, and these included a new engine, new fire-control, night-vision and navigation systems, and add-on suites of passive armour. In this way the life of the vehicle was extended until the Arjun came into service.

Some 2,200 Vijayantas were built before production ceased. Other countries who also bought the Vickers Mark 1 included Kuwait, who purchased 70 from 1970–72.

BELOW: **In the late 1950s India was looking to replace their ageing Centurions, which had done so well in the Indo-Pakistan wars against the American-built Pakistani tanks, due mainly to their simpler fire-control systems. They decided upon the Vickers Mark 1, which they called Vijayanta (Victory). Vickers built the first 90 in order to meet the agreed production deadline, the rest of the order being manufactured in India at a new factory in Madras. Many of the 2,000 fleet remain in service, despite being supplemented or replaced by more modern Russian MBTs, some of which are locally built.**

ABOVE: **The Kartik AVLB is based upon the lengthened chassis of the Vijayanta, which is also used for the Catapult SP artillery system.**

Vickers Mark 3 Main Battle Tank

An upgrade of the Mark 1 with changes to the hull, a new engine and a new turret, the Vickers Mark 3 MBT first appeared as an export model in 1977. Weighing 38,700kg/38.1 tons and fitted with a torsion bar suspension system, it was powered by a Detroit Diesel 12V-71T engine, giving it a top speed of 50kph/31.1mph and a range of 530km/329.3 miles. The vehicle's armament remained the same as its predecessor, the 105mm/4.13in L7A1 main gun and two 7.62mm/0.3in machine-guns (one coaxial), but mounted in a newly designed steel turret, with a reloading port on the left-hand side and a commander's cupola and hatch for the loader on the turret top. Fifty rounds of main gun ammunition were carried – 18 in the turret itself and a further 32 in the hull. Other changes included up-rated fire-control, night-vision, NBC (Nuclear, Biological and Chemical) protection, communication and safety systems, making the Mark 3 an infinitely more sophisticated weapon system than the Mark 1.

Another version developed for sale to Malaysia included an ERA (Explosive Reactive Armour) armour package and a GPS (Global Positioning System) Satellite Navigation (SatNav) system, as well as a range of further optional enhancement packages.

LEFT, ABOVE AND ABOVE RIGHT: **The next Vickers MBT was the Mark 3, of similar weight and size to the Mark 1, with a 105mm/4.13in gun, complete with laser rangefinder. The first Mark 3 production order was placed in 1977 by Kenya, followed by Nigeria. Sadly, others did not follow.**

Vickers Mark 3 MBT	
Entered service: 1977	
Crew: 4	
Weight: 38,700kg/38.1 tons	
Dimensions: Length – 7.56m/24ft 9.5in	
Height (over turret hatch) – 2.48m/8ft 1.5in	
Width – 3.17m/10ft 5in	
Armament: Main – 105mm/4.13in L7A1 gun	
Secondary – 2 x 7.62mm/0.3in and	
1 x 12.7mm/0.5in machine-guns	
Armour: Maximum – 80mm/3.15in	
Powerplant: Detroit Diesel 12V-71T diesel,	
536.9kW/720bhp	
Performance: Speed – 50kph/31.1mph	
Range – 530km/329.3 miles	

Vickers VFM Mark 5 Light Tank

The VFM Mark 5 was first seen in 1986 at the British Army Equipment Exhibition (BAEE), and was another AFV developed by Vickers for the export market. The vehicle was developed in conjunction with an American company – FMC – using its Close Combat Vehicle (Light) or CCV(L) as the basis on which to mount a turret containing British armament. This produced a light tank with a considerable punch.

Weighing 19,750kg/19.4 tons with welded aluminium armour, the VFM was powered by a modular Detroit Diesel V6 turbocharged engine, delivering a top speed of 70kph/43.5mph and a range of 480km/298.3 miles. The power pack is housed in the distinctly raised rear hull and fitted with a ramp door to enable speedy access. The turret echoes the rising hull by also tapering at its rear, while mounting the L7 105mm/4.13in smoothbore main gun, along with two 7.62mm/0.3in machine-guns.

Designed to be air-portable in both the C130 Hercules and C141 Starlifter transport aircraft, it could also be dropped using the Low Altitude Parachute Extraction System (LAPES).

ABOVE LEFT, ABOVE AND BELOW LEFT: **The Vickers VFM 5 was a 19,750kg/19.4-ton light tank that was a joint venture between Vickers Defence Systems and the FMC Corporation of USA. The first prototype was on show at the 1986 BAEE, and a year later it had completed its firing and mobility trials. It was designed to be air-portable in both the C130 Hercules and the C141 Starlifter transport aircraft, and to be dropped by LAPES (Low Altitude Parachute Extraction System). It did not find a market, so never went into full production.**

Vickers VFM Mark 5 Light Tank

Entered service: 1987
Crew: 4
Weight: 19,750kg/19.4 tons
Dimensions: Length – 6.20m/20ft 4in
    Height (over turret hatch) – 2.62m/8ft 7in
    Width – 2.69m/8ft 10in
Armament: Main – 105mm/4.13in L7 gun
    Secondary – 2 x 7.62mm/0.3in machine-guns
Armour: Unspecified
Powerplant: Detroit Diesel V6, 739.9kW/992hp
Performance: Speed – 70kph/43.5mph
    Range – 480km/298.3 miles

Vickers Mark 7 Valiant Main Battle Tank

Originally developed as a technology demonstrator at the same time as the VFM Mark 5, the Vickers Mark 7 Valiant represented another strand in the dynamic export market push of the mid-1980s undertaken by Vickers. This time the development partner was Germany and the resulting Vickers Mark 7 was even more versatile than its Mark 5 predecessor in being able to port a wide variety of European-manufactured equipment. Using British composite armour (known as Chobham after the town where it was developed) and a British turret, combined with a German chassis, engine and running gear (essentially the bottom of the Kraus-Maffei-built Leopard 2), the Valiant could mount a variety of main guns. The first option was the British rifled 120mm/4.72in L11A5, the second a French Giat

CN 120-26 120mm/4.72in, and the third a German Rheinmetall smoothbore 120mm/4.72in.

The vehicle is also fitted with the Marconi Centaur integrated gun and fire control as well as navigation, NBC (Nuclear, Biological and Chemical) protection and fire-suppression systems. The Mark 7 Valiant was overtaken by events (the first

ABOVE, LEFT AND BELOW LEFT: **Shortly after news of the development of the revolutionary Chobham armour in 1976, details were passed to Vickers, and the following year it was decided to produce a Chobham-armoured MBT weighing 54,640kg/53.4 tons, to be called the Vickers Mark 7 MBT (Valiant). Unfortunately Valiant was overtaken by events and never went further than the prototype stage. However, it did provide much useful experience in the production of a Chobham-armoured tank, which would eventually lead on to Challenger.**

Gulf War of the early 1990s) and never went into production, but it did provide much useful experience, which led to the development of the Vickers Challenger 2 MBT.

Vickers Mark 7 Valiant MBT	

Entered service: 1985
Crew: 4
Weight: 54,640kg/53.4 tons
Dimensions: Length – 7.72m/25ft 4in
   Height (over turret hatch) – 2.54m/8ft 4in
   Width – 3.42m/11ft 2.5in
Armament: Main – 120mm/4.72in L11A5 gun
   Secondary – 2 x 7.62mm/0.3in machine-guns
Armour: Unspecified
Powerplant: MTU MB873 V12 diesel, delivering
   1,118.6kW/1,500hp
Performance: Speed – 72kph/44.7mph
   Range – 550km/343.75 miles

Glossary

AEV Armoured Engineer Vehicle – AFV based upon an MBT chassis, crewed by engineers with the equipment to carry out engineering tasks.

AFV Armoured Fighting Vehicle – any armoured vehicle, whether tracked or wheeled, normally carrying an offensive weapon.

AP Armour-Piercing – ammunition that will penetrate armour plate rather than shatter or glance off on striking it.

APC Armoured Personnel Carrier – an AFV primarily designed to carry a number of fully equipped infantry soldiers.

APDS Armour-Piercing Discarding Sabot – a form of AP with a small, heavy core surrounded by a calibre-sized casing, which breaks up on leaving the gun muzzle. The core then flies on to the target with added velocity.

APFSDS Armour-Piercing Fin-Stabilized Discarding Sabot – the same as APDS but with a longer, finned core to give better penetration.

ARV Armoured Recovery Vehicle – an AFV based on a tank chassis, crewed by fitters with the equipment to carry out the repair and recovery of most AFVs.

automatic gun A weapon that loads, fires, extracts, ejects and reloads continually while the firing mechanism is engaged and the feed mechanism supplies ammunition.

automatic loader A mechanism which, together with some form of magazine or dispenser, allows for automatic loading of a tank gun, thus dispensing with one crew member.

AVLB Armoured Vehicle Launched Bridge – an AFV based upon a tank chassis, normally crewed by engineers and carrying some type of vehicular bridge.

AVRE Armoured Vehicle Royal Engineers – British nomenclature for an AEV.

ball mount A spherical machine-gun mount permitting firing in various directions.

BARV Beach Armoured Recovery Vehicle – an ARV specially designed to recover "drowned" AFVs and keep exits from landing craft clear during assault landings.

bogie Units of a tank's suspension that help to distribute the sprung weight along the track.

calibre The diameter of the bore of a gun.

chassis That part of the tank that makes it mobile as opposed to the part for fighting.

coaxial The mounting of two weapons in the same mount.

cradle The non-recoiling part of the gun mount that allows elevation of the gun about the trunnions, houses the recoil system and guides it in recoil.

cupola A small protuberance above the main turret, equipped with vision devices and a protective lid, mainly for use by the tank commander.

ERA Explosive Reactive Armour – explosive plates attached to the outside of a tank that explode outwards when struck, thus negating penetration.

fascine A large bundle of pieces of wood (or nowadays metal pipes) carried on an AFV to be dropped into a ditch or hole to enable the tank to cross.

fume extractor A device fitted to the barrel of a tank gun to enable the gases remaining behind after firing to be sucked out of the muzzle before the breech is opened, so that they do not enter the turret during reloading.

FV Fighting Vehicle, usually plus a number – British Defence Department nomenclature for British-built AFVs.

glacis plate The thick armour plate at the front of a tank, normally sloped at an angle so as to deflect enemy shot.

hatch An opening complete with cover and often vision devices, giving access in and out by crew members.

HE High-Explosive – the standard bursting explosive.

HEAT High-Explosive Anti-Tank – a type of projectile with a shaped charge that concentrates the explosion into a thin jet enabling it to penetrate armour plate.

HESH High-Explosive Squash-Head – HE filled with plastic explosive that "squashes" on the armour plate before exploding, blowing a "scab" of metal off the inside surface rather than penetrating.

idler The undriven guide wheel carrying the tank track.

mantlet The moveable piece of armour plate that surrounds the hole into which the main armament is fitted into the turret. This hole has to be large enough to allow the gun to elevate and depress. It both protects and conceals this opening.

MBT Main Battle Tank – since World War II this term has been used to cover all types of modern medium and heavy tanks, from about 30,481kg/30 tons upwards to 60,963kg/60 tons and over. MBT is in essence the modern-day term for the British Universal Tank.

NBC Nuclear, Biological and Chemical.

rifling The spiral grooves in the bore of the gun that impart accuracy and stability to a projectile in flight.

semi-automatic gun A gun that requires the trigger to be pulled for each round fired.

separated ammunition Ammunition that requires separate loading of the projectile, propelling charge and primer.

skirting plates or side skirts Sheets of thin armour that hang in front of the upper run of the tracks and suspension. These cause HEAT projectiles to explode and thus dissipate their main force before reaching the hull.

SPAT Self-Propelled Anti-Tank – an anti-tank gun mounted on either wheels or tracks with an engine, so that it does not need a towing vehicle.

sponson A projection mounting a weapon, located upon a tank hull.

sprocket A toothed wheel which engages with the track to drive it, and is itself driven by the engine.

suspension The wheels, tracks, rollers, roadwheels, bogies etc, on which the tank runs.

TD Tank Destroyer – a self-propelled anti-tank gun on a similar chassis to a tank but normally with lighter armour and an open top.

track The part of a tank that is in contact with the ground and is guided by the idler, sprocket and top rollers.

Index

Acknowledgements

The author would like to thank the staff of the Tank Museum, Bovington, especially David Fletcher, Janice Tait and Roland Groom, for all their help.

The publisher would like to thank the following for the use of their pictures in the book (l=left, r=right, t=top, b=bottom, m=middle). Every effort has been made to acknowledge the pictures properly; however, we apologize if there are any unintentional omissions, which will be corrected in future editions.

© Crown Copyright/MOD. Reproduced with the permission of the Controller of Her Majesty's Stationery Office: 7tl; 7tr; 21b; 34b; 45t; 45m; 46b; 47m.

Simon Dunstan: 12t; 12b; 13t (US Army); 13m (US Army); 13b (US Marine Corps); 31tr; 40t; 58t; 58b; 59br; 65tl; 65m; 67t; 67m; 73ml.

David Eshel: 16t; 16b; 17tl; 17tr; 17b; 29m; 36b; 57t; 79t; 79b; 80t; 80b; 81t; 81m; 81b; 86t; 90t; 90m; 90b; 97t; 97m; 97b.

Bob Fleming: 100b.

George Forty: 10t; 11bl; 11br; 14; 15tr; 18l; 18r; 20; 21tl; 21tr; 21mr; 24b; 34m; 35b; 38m; 43t; 64t; 71t; 71b; 77b; 78tr; 83t; 83m; 83b; 84t; 84b; 89b; 91t; 124b.

Christopher F. Foss: 32t; 32b; 33t; 33b; 34t; 40b (Indian MoD); 41m; 41b; 43b; 52b; 60t; 60m; 60b; 61t; 73tr; 75t; 75b; 88t; 88b; 93b; 98b; 106m; 110t; 110b; 111t; 111b; 113b; 114b; 115b; 117m; 117b; 118; 119t; 119b; 121t; 122bl; 122br.

General Dynamics Land Systems Division: 6b; 30t; 31m.

Richard P. Hunnicutt: 69b; 74t (US Army); 82m (US Army); 82b (US Army).

RTR Publications Trust: 6t; 7b; 23tr; 23b; 24t; 25tr; 44b; 45b; 46t; 47t; 47b.

The Tank Museum, Bovington: 1, 2, 3, 4, 8–9; 10b; 11t; 15tl; 15m; 15b; 19tl; 19tr; 19b; 22tl; 22–3t; 22b; 25tl; 25bl; 25br; 26–7; 28t; 28b; 29t; 29b;

31tl; 35t; 35m; 36t; 37t; 37m; 37b; 38t; 39t; 42t; 42b; 44t; 48t; 48b; 49t; 49m; 49b; 50t; 50b; 51t; 51b; 52t; 53t; 53m; 53b; 54t; 54b; 55t; 55b; 56t; 56m; 56b; 57m; 57b; 62t; 64b; 65tr; 65t; 66t; 66b; 67b; 68t; 68b; 69t; 69m; 70t; 70b; 71m; 72t; 72b; 73tl; 76t; 76b; 77t; 77ml; 77mr; 78tl; 78b; 82t; 86b; 87tl; 87tr; 87b; 89t; 91b; 93m; 94t; 94b; 95t; 95m; 95b; 96t; 96b; 98; 98m; 99t; 99m; 99b; 100t; 101tl; 101tr; 101m; 101b; 102t; 102bl; 102br; 104t; 104b; 105ml; 105mr; 105b; 106t; 106b; 107t; 107b; 108t; 108b; 109t; 109m; 109b; 112t; 112m; 112b; 113t; 113m; 114t; 115t; 115m; 116t; 116b; 117t; 120t; 120b; 121b; 122t; 123t; 123bl; 123br; 124tl; 124tr; 125t; 125m; 125b; 127; 128t; 128b.

TRH Pictures: 38b; 39m; 39b; 41t; 59t; 59bl; 61b; 62b; 63tl; 63tr; 63m; 63b; 74b; 85t; 85m; 85b; 92t; 92b; 93t; 103t; 103m; 103b.

US Army: 30b; 31b; 73b; 105t.